How to do a Research Project

WITHDRAWN

How to do a Research Project

A guide for undergraduate students

Second Edition

Colin Robson

WILEY

Registered office

John Wiley & Sons Ltd, The Atrium, Southern Gate, Chichester, West Sussex, PO19 8SQ, United Kingdom

For details of our global editorial offices, for customer services and for information about how to apply for permission to reuse the copyright material in this book please see our website at www.wiley.com.

Library of Congress Cataloging-in-Publication Data

Robson, Colin.
   How to do a research project : a guide for undergraduate students / Colin Robson. – Second Edition.
      pages cm
   Includes bibliographical references and index.
   ISBN 978-1-118-69132-8 (pbk. : alk. paper)   1.   Report writing.   2.   Social sciences–Research. 3.   Research–Methodology.   4.   Project method in teaching.   I. Title.
   LB2369.R575 2014
   808.02–dc23

                                                                                                    2014020566

              ISBN: 978-1-118-69132-8 (pbk)
              ISBN: 978-1-118-91616-2 (ebk)
              ISBN: 978-1-118-91621-6 (ebk)

      A catalogue record for this book is available from the British Library.

      Set in 10/12pt LegacySerifStd-Book by Thomson Digital, Noida, India

      Printed in Great Britain by TJ International Ltd, Padstow, Cornwall

Contents

Contents

Preface

Carrying out a research project (sometimes referred to as a dissertation or thesis) is an important part of many undergraduate degree courses in UK universities. It is usually in the final year and can make a substantial contribution to the honours class awarded. This has been less common in US institutions although there is a strong trend to make it a 'capstone' (i.e. a crowning achievement) of the senior or final year of an undergraduate degree.

This book concentrates on projects where the research focus is on people, typically where social research methods such as interviews, or question-naires, or some kind of observation is used. In academic discipline terms this covers courses in the various social sciences. Projects in applied fields such as education, areas related to health including nursing, and social work and many others, also commonly use these methods. However, much of the material in the book is directly relevant to any undergraduate research project.

In traditional degree courses the final year research project was very different from the rest of the programme. Whereas that was made up, very largely or exclusively, of taught tutor-led components the project was an important piece of work for which all students were individually responsi-ble. Also, traditionally, written examinations were dominant and so the final year project presented a relatively unfamiliar type of assessment. Many students reported feeling considerable stress and anxiety both when antici-pating, and in carrying out, the project.

Changes in the structure and curriculum of first degrees, mean that the context of many final year research projects has changed. Increasing recognition of the importance of research methods and methodology, and recent developments in both qualitative and quantitative aspects, have led to the provision of substantial taught courses which help prepare students for the research project.

Course work is now widely used as a component of assessment rather than there being an exclusive reliance on formal examinations. It helps develop skills in information gathering, writing and referencing useful in the research project. There is also, in many institutions an effort to develop independence in student learning throughout the degree programme, rather than the final year research project being uniquely different.

Developments like this will better prepare you for the project but they are by no means universal. In any case, because of the project's importance, some trepidation is inevitable. The good news is that many students find it the most interesting and exciting part of the whole degree course. You have the opportunity of finding out something new, different from what anyone has done previously. And in doing this you have demonstrated a whole set of useful skills which will stand you in good stead while applying for, and carrying out, a wide range of jobs. The quotations in Box 0.1 are typical.

Box 0.1 Undergraduate views about the research project/dissertation

'My dissertation is probably the most useful thing I have ever written at university. I doubt I'll ever have to write an essay again, but if I do have to write reports, it'll be in the same form as my dissertation.'

'From Level one I had dreaded the prospect of doing what seemed a huge piece of work, but with hindsight I feel that the support given along the way has resulted in a dissertation better than I thought I could do.'

'I valued this piece of work as it was a presentation of all the skills I had developed whilst being in education.'

'Felt that I learnt as much about myself as I did about the topic.'

'Probably the toughest piece of work done solely due to gaining confidence to collect data and time management.'

'There is no doubting completing my dissertation was one of the most stressful times of my life but at the same time the most rewarding.'

'I enjoyed having the chance to show what I am capable of. I found it very stressful at times, but achieved huge sense of satisfaction when over.'

Source: Harrison, M.E., & Whalley, W.B. (2008). Undertaking a dissertation from start to finish: The process and product, *Journal of Geography in Higher Education*, 32(3), 401–418. p.408

Remember also that you are not alone. A project supervisor or tutor should provide you with help and advice. Increases in student numbers and pressures on university finances mean that, realistically, this may be severely limited. Find out what you can expect and make sure that you take full advantage of what is on offer. Some universities have decided that they can no longer afford to offer a final year project as part of the degree. Presumably, if you are reading this book, your institution shares my view that it is well worth its place.

I believe that the basics of carrying out this type of research project are the same for all disciplines and areas of study. It is sometimes suggested that research is some kind of elite activity that few are capable of taking part in. I disagree. Certainly, any student who has made it through to the final year of a degree course should be capable of completing a successful research project. It is not easy, but with effort and organization, and by taking advantage of the help available within your institution, and the advice in this book, you will be well equipped for the task.

If, as is the case with many degrees, you have already completed one or more courses on research methods before focusing on your research project, the material on the background to using social research methods in Chapter 2 will provide a reminder. If not, the further reading suggested will provide the introduction you need. Chapter 2 also includes examples of reports by undergraduate students based on their own projects and published in journals of undergraduate research. They have been selected to illustrate both the wide range of possible approaches (pp. 24–31) and the similarly wide range of methods of collecting data (pp. 40–46) that can be used. While they are likely to be indicative of some of the better work produced by undergraduates, they show what is feasible at this level. And their diversity could encourage you to 'think outside the box' when you are developing your ideas for a research topic.

Acknowledgements

I am very grateful to the many students and colleagues at Birkbeck University of London, the University of Huddersfield, and the former Hester Adrian Research Centre, University of Manchester who have, in various ways, contributed to my education as a writer. I give particular thanks to the late Professor Brian Foss who, many years ago, encouraged me to turn lecture notes prepared for University of London Summer Schools in Experimental Psychology into a text on research design, which first set me on the writing route.

I would like to put on record, on behalf of anyone involved with undergraduate research projects, my thanks for the wealth of useful material now freely available on the internet. Sites such as Bill Trochim's 'Web Center for Social Research Methods' (http://www.socialresearchmethods.net/), and the 'Guide to Undergraduate Dissertations in the Social Sciences' (http://www.socscidiss.bham.ac.uk/), coordinated by Malcolm Todd from Sheffield Hallam University, are examples to us all.

In similar vein I commend the growth of journals devoted to undergraduate research, mainly linked to universities in the United States but more recently in the United Kingdom and other countries. I would like to give particular mention to 'Reinvention: An International Journal of Undergraduate Research' (http://www2.warwick.ac.uk/fac/cross_fac/iatl/reinvention) published initially by the University of Warwick in the United Kingdom, but now in association with Monash University in Australia. I consider it to be a model of the genre in its openness to contributions from many institutions and disciplines, and its principled open-access and professional standard website (evidenced by my many citations of Reinvention papers in Chapter 2, Boxes 2.2 and 2.4).

I remain indebted to my wife Pat for her sage advice on written style – and for many other, more important, things in life.

Introduction

Carrying out a research project or dissertation forms an important part of many undergraduate degree courses. This book covers what you need to think about and do to deliver a successful project. The focus is on projects where data are collected using methods such as interviews, questionnaires or some type of observation – commonly called social research methods. It concentrates on the issues involved and on the range of possibilities you might consider. Examples are provided based on projects carried out by undergraduate students.

There is a general checklist on p. 6 of the things you will need to cover when planning the project. Extensive annotated lists of further reading are included at the end of each chapter and in other places in the text. I have also incorporated links to substantial amounts of additional material in the website associated with the book, www.wiley.com/college/robson.

How to do a Research Project addresses the needs of undergraduates following those disciplines and applied fields where social research methods are commonly used, including:

☐ business and management studies
☐ education
☐ health-related areas
☐ psychology
☐ social anthropology

☐ social work and social policy
☐ sociology, and
☐ sport and leisure studies.

It is also directly relevant to projects in other fields[*] where, while it is not the norm for students to use these methods, they are needed to answer particular research questions.

This book concentrates on research where the focus is on people: what they do and how we can understand what is going on. My own background is as a psychologist, working mainly in applied fields such as education and health-related areas. However, the basics of doing people-focused research seem to me to have many characteristics in common, whatever the field. What does differ from field to field are the expectations, assumptions and traditions of researchers. While you will need to take note of this (discussed under the heading of 'Considering your audience' in Chapter 1, p. 11, and Chapter 6, p. 136), the first-time researcher can bring to the task freshness of vision and absence of preconceptions.

The focus is on small-scale research – a project that you can complete from start to finish in a couple of months at the outside – although the particular features of some small projects may spread it out over longer.

My aim is to give you the confidence to complete a worthwhile project. This need not be a very difficult technical task, but it does call for:

☐ organisation (sorting out what you have to do)
☐ commitment (actually doing it) and, in many projects,
☐ good social skills (getting on with people, not upsetting them or getting their backs up).

All projects must fulfil two crucial criteria. First, that they are *feasible*. They can be completed with the resources, including time, that you have available. Secondly, that they are *ethical*. The project will not cause harm to those involved or others.

Research depends on getting hold of some information or data and doing something with it. A central message of this book is that the type of information or data you need to collect is largely determined by the

---

[*] For example architecture, art and design, catering and hospitality studies, communication and media studies, computer sciences, conflict and peace studies, criminology, development studies, economics, environmental studies, geography, history, information sciences, legal studies, linguistics, literary studies, media studies, music, planning, political science, religious studies, tourism, and urban design.

questions to which you seek answers – known, unsurprisingly, as the research questions. Sorting this out is the main task in Chapter 3.

The suggestions for further reading at the end of chapters allow you to follow up issues of direct relevance to your own project. They are annotated, with short descriptions of what you might get from each one. I've tried to select, whenever possible, up-to-date books which are readily available and not hideously expensive. The website associated with the text provides suggestions for discipline-specific further reading and links to material supporting the discussion of issues covered in the book itself.

The Internet and Your Project

For anyone doing research at any level, or in any discipline or field of study, the internet is such a powerful information resource that anyone not taking advantage of its existence is severely and unnecessarily handicapping themselves. In particular, those fortunate persons, such as undergraduate students, with access to the resources of an academic library have a gateway to almost unimaginable riches. Most obviously, this is through systems giving access to journal articles, such as the United Kingdom's 'Open Athens' scheme (http://www.eduserv.org.uk/services/OpenAthens) and similar schemes in other countries. You should be taking full advantage of all such internet resources available through your institution.

For researchers using social research methods, the internet has also had a substantial influence on how data are collected in many projects. There is an ease of access to people via e-mail and other web-based systems not possible using traditional methods. The internet itself is increasingly seen as an important focus for social research. For example, the central part that social media play in many people's lives throughout the world has understandably attracted much research interest.

The digital world we all live in now produces opportunities for rethinking both the approaches taken by researchers and the methods appropriate for collecting data. See Roberts, Hine, Morey, Snee & Watson (2013), especially the case studies on pp. 8–18, if you would like to take this further.

The undoubted advantages that use of the internet brings must be balanced by an appreciation of its shortcomings and potential dangers in research terms. There is a preponderance of dross and material of dubious quality, highlighting the need for students to develop skills in assessing quality. Finally, using the internet either as a tool for data collection or as a topic for research, brings new ethical challenges for researchers.

The role of the internet in research projects, together with problems and issues, is mainly dealt with in Chapter 3.

You will get more from this book if you follow the links in the book (otherwise known as URLs), including those in the 'References and author index' (p. 145) - and to those in the book's website. They add significantly to the text and demonstrate what is available on the internet for a researcher.[†]

A note on language

To avoid giving the impression that all researchers and others mentioned are female (or male), and disliking the 'she/he' approach, I use the plural 'they' whenever possible. If the singular can't be avoided, I use 'he' and 'she' more or less randomly.

[†] Paragraphs in italics like this flag what I consider important material, or things which I find can worry or confuse students.

PART I

Making Preparations

This first part is about preliminary planning. It covers the things that you need to think about in the early stages of working on your project. Doing a research project is rather like house painting and decorating – prepare thoroughly and you will reap the rewards later.

The project planning checklist overleaf provides an overview. The following chapters discuss the issues involved in detail. There is a set of suggested tasks at the end of each chapter to help you plan.

Box I.1 Project planning checklist

1. Know the Rules

Before committing yourself, you need to know the realities of your situation. What kind of project is expected? What kind of report? How long? When is the deadline? See Chapter 1, pp. 9–10.

2. Know the Social Research Methods You Might Use

Researchers have developed a wide range of general approaches and methods of collecting data when doing projects involving people. It helps to know the range of possibilities open to you. See Chapter 2, pp. 24–31 and 40–46.

3. Decide on a Topic

What general topic or research area interests you? Discuss possibilities with your supervisor, fellow students and others who might help. Use sources of information (people, books, journals, internet, etc.) to confirm, or change, your choice of topic. See Chapter 3, pp. 59-63.

Note: You will also have to use sources when sorting out each of the following topics:

4. Decide on the Research Questions

Come up with a small number of questions to which your research will plan to produce answers. These questions may be modified as you get further into your planning. See Chapter 3, pp. 63-66.

5. Decide on the Design

Consider what general approach, and which method or methods of data collection, will provide answers to these questions. Review Chapter 2, pp. 22-54.

6. Consider Ethical Issues

Give serious attention to possible ethical issues arising from your proposed research, and work out how they will be dealt with. See Chapter 3, pp. 74-77.

7. Obtain Any Necessary Approvals for Access

Seek approval, at the earliest possible date, from whoever is responsible. See Chapter 4, pp. 91-93.

8. Draw Up a Project Outline and Timetable

List all the stages which you need to go through to do the research and end up with a completed project report. Produce a realistic timetable. See Chapter 4, pp. 101–104.

1

Preliminaries

Recognizing Realities

The realities of your situation will strongly influence what you can do. For example:

- [ ] *What are the course requirements?* You need to know the formal specification for the project, often provided in a handbook. What type of project is expected – do you collect your own data or is a 'library' study expected? How and when is it to be presented – length, format, etc.? The general rule is – if they say 'these are the rules', then you follow them. There may be room for negotiation or interpretation if you feel that some aspect isn't appropriate for the project you want to do – but you must get this agreed before proceeding.

- [ ] *What are the expectations of your supervisor?* You should have access to a member of staff who provides help and support with your project, often called a supervisor. These people are human beings, and as such, will have their own preferences, expectations and even prejudices about what makes a good project. While the obvious strategy is to go along with them, the good supervisor should welcome your initiative if you come up with something different. If they are not amenable to your suggested approach, do remember that the supervisor will almost inevitably have substantially more experience than you. Follow their suggestions. With the experience of completing this project behind you, you will be in a better position to decide for yourself when you do later research.

- [ ] *What can you expect from your supervisor?* The amount of individual contact time that you can expect should be clearly specified. Three to four hours, spread out over the period you are working on the project, appear typical. Keep your appointments and prepare for them, armed with questions, problems and issues you want to discuss.

☐ *Can the project be linked to your job or to one you are aiming for after your degree course?* In many professional courses, such links are the norm and will be organized by your supervisor. If you have come on to a course from a job in an organization which you plan to return to after the degree, or are doing the degree part time while keeping the job, it makes sense to link the project to the needs of the organization. This puts you in a strong position because it is in their interest to give you the support needed to enable you to carry out the project. You need to know why they want the work done, mainly so that you can frame the project in such a way that it stands a chance of answering their questions. But it is also so that you can satisfy yourself you aren't being asked to do something unethical (see 'Avoiding the unethical' Chapter 3, p. 76).

A serious warning

One of the commonest problems of novice researchers (and of experienced ones who should know better) is biting off more than they can chew. They under-estimate how long things take and over-estimate what they can do, with the time and resources that they have available.

Making it Worthwhile

Two main things make doing a research project worthwhile for you. First, completing it. Secondly, the skills and experience you gain from doing it. Completing it (which includes writing a report) helps justify the time and effort that you have put into it. An unfinished project means that you have effectively wasted your time, as well as the time of the people who have taken part.

Doing a project calls for a wide range of skills and gives valuable experience. These include:

☐ *process skills* – such as problem formulation and solving, use of data collection techniques, data analysis, etc.
☐ *presentation skills* – such as report writing, data presentation, audience awareness, etc.
☐ *management skills* – such as project planning, time management, working with others, etc., and
☐ *personal skills* – such as self-discipline, originality, ability to learn, acceptance of criticism, etc.

All of these can, of course, be made much of in your résumé or CV.

A successfully completed project puts you in a position to do better and bigger further projects. It is not uncommon for doctoral and other post-graduate research to have its roots in this first small-scale project. Mistakes and blunders can provide useful learning experiences. They will be etched on your mind, making their repetition highly unlikely (you will just make different mistakes – nobody is perfect!).

Be wary of using people as 'research-fodder'. If people take part in your project and give you time and attention, you should seek to make it worthwhile for them. This can be through:

☐ *Giving feedback.* The deal you agree when asking others to take part in your project (see Chapter 4, p. 91) should normally involve you undertaking to let them know something about your findings.

☐ *Letting them talk.* People are often pleased by someone showing an interest in them and relish the opportunity of talking to an interested person about themselves. So, don't just cut and run when you think that you have what you need for the project. Their spontaneous comments can be more interesting than the answers to your carefully crafted questions.

Considering Your Audience(s)

In one sense, you carry out the project for yourself, perhaps because you want to find out or understand something. One good reason is because it will help you gain a qualification, or further your career. However, other people come into the picture. You can think of them as audiences for your research. This is most obvious in relation to the report you will produce. Your examiners are a crucial audience. There will be a formal specification and you must make sure that you know what this is and stick to it. If it says 10,000 words, you stay very close to that limit.

Some research carries with it the notion, implicitly or explicitly, that, by carrying it out, you might help to change and improve some situation. It may be appropriate for you to provide a different, additional, report to that needed for the degree award. Perhaps something written for a senior management team in a business, or a report seeking to communicate with volunteers at a centre for young persons with learning difficulties. These issues are returned to in the final chapter.

Bearing audiences in mind is important at all stages of the project. Your supervisor forms an audience you want to please. If you are doing the research linked to your job, it is essential that you find out what your boss or line manager is expecting from the project. And that you plan something which could deliver this (or carry out a subtle re-education process where you persuade them that there is a better way).

To get the active support that you need to carry out a successful project in an organization, it will help not only to have the top brass on your side, but also to be doing something which is potentially helpful to the workers (see the section on gaining access in Chapter 4, p. 91. More generally, whoever act as participants* in your study constitute an audience to take note of. Your interactions with them should show respect and consideration for their likely sensitivities.

Considering these multiple audiences influences the nature of your project. Some audiences only respect quantitative, statistical evidence. Others would take more note of rich qualitative data. If you have to satisfy both kinds of audience, you might have to use more than one method or approach, and possibly produce different reports for them. There is increasing interest in such 'mixed-method' projects.

Individual or Group Research?

There is much to be said in favour of collaborating with others when carrying out a research project. Research is very commonly a group activity and demonstrating that you have acquired the skills of working successfully with others is another marketable asset. However, many degree course regulations either insist on individual projects, or set strict limits on the type of collaboration which is allowed. Check this out.

Types of group research

Group research can take many forms:

☐ Forming a group with fellow students or colleagues where the research is jointly designed, carried out, and reported on. Decisions are reached via consensus. It is not an easy option, and is very risky unless you and the other group members have already got successful experience of working in this way. This approach is rarely permitted by course regulations, in part because of the difficulty in assessing the individual contributions of group members.
☐ Forming a group where several people are interested in the same broad topic and, through discussion, carve out related projects. Details of the design and other aspects of each project are the responsibility of the individual concerned, with other members of the group giving advice

---

* The term 'participant' is now widely used to refer to those taking part in a research project, rather than 'subject'. See Chapter 4, p. 86 for a discussion of this issue.

and support at all stages. The quality of your project is likely to be enhanced by linking the discussion, and findings, to those of other group members. Providing that you clearly signal which parts are your own work and which that of others, it would be unreasonable for course regulations to prohibit this form of group working (but they might do).

☐ Forming a group with persons having a role in the setting where your research takes place. This applies particularly when your project involves evaluating a programme, intervention, innovation, or whatever, where there is much advantage in involving the personnel concerned. For example, a project which is focused on problems and issues which they feel are important, is much more likely to get their active cooperation than trying to persuade them to go along with your own pet ideas (see Robson, 2000; Chapter 2, for more details about the advantages of this kind of collaboration in evaluation research).

Support groups

Even when everyone wants to do their own thing, and the proposed topics are very various, forming a mutual support group is well worthwhile. Group members will have different strengths and perspectives and will be able to offer comments. Towards the completion of the project, reading of each other's draft reports is very valuable. It is a good idea to agree ground rules for the group at an early stage – see Box 1.1.

Box 1.1 Issues for support groups

☐ Do you need/want a leader/organizer? If so –

   ☐ What are their responsibilities (e.g. calling meetings; moderator; keeping records)? and
   ☐ Does the role rotate?

☐ Do you have an agenda with pre-circulated material – or free discussion?

It is good to have:

☐ Regular meetings with attendance accepted as a priority, and
☐ Agreement to keep to constructive criticism and comments.

Supervisor support. If, for whatever reasons, you are forced to do an individual project, don't despair. Your supervisor should be a major resource. They want their students to succeed (partly, though hopefully not solely, because it can take a lot of their effort to help get an unsatisfactory project up to standard). If you are not getting the support you are entitled to, there should be mechanisms for remedying the situation. Be reasonable though. They are busy people and you have your part of the bargain to fulfil through attendance and involvement. Some institutions have moved toward small-group rather than individual supervision sessions with promising results, partly because they provide a setting where students can discuss each other's work and provide mutual support (Akister, Williams & Maynard, 2009).

Web-based discussion and other groups. You could also consider ways of getting involved in, or forming, a group via the internet. There is a myriad of discussion groups and other web entities through which you can get advice, and possibly also get in touch with persons in a similar situation as yourself. I have been very impressed by the way in which established researchers are willing to give advice to those less experienced, in discussion groups on a wide range of research-related topics. The usual warnings and safeguards about internet activities apply (see Chapter 3, p. 69).

Planning Your Project

The checklist on p. 6 provides a set of planning milestones. It is self-evident that you need to sort out a focus or *topic* for your project. Coming up with a set of non-trivial *research questions*, which are answerable given the time and resources you have available, is a very useful way of giving a shape to your efforts.

Your *research design* is the way you have chosen to try to get answers to these research questions. This includes the research methods, such as questionnaires, interviews, observation, documentary analysis, etc., which you decide to use. It also refers to your overall approach to the research. There are very different styles, or strategies, of research ranging from a tightly controlled experimental design collecting quantitative (numerical) data, to ethnographic approaches relying on participant observation and producing largely qualitative (non-numerical, usually verbal) data.

Once you have a clear idea of your research questions and design, you can give serious attention to the ethical issues which could arise and seek any approvals for access needed without delay. When these issues are settled satisfactorily, you are in a position to draw up your project outline and timetable listing all the stages needed to complete the project.

Doing it

After planning comes action. You move on to actual data or information collection. Reliance on existing information (sometimes referred to as documentary analysis, or library research) is a fully legitimate form of research activity and is the norm in some fields or discipline. However, much research involves active data collection (sometimes referred to as primary data collection), whether inside or outside a specialist laboratory. Non-laboratory, or 'field' research, has its own challenges which often call for good social skills, as well as skills in using the research methods.

Writing the project report is an essential part of the whole exercise. However, before you can write it, you need to know what you have found. Collected data typically do not speak for themselves. You have to make them talk. This process of achieving understanding of what you have found through analysis and interpretation is often presented as difficult and highly technical. It can be, and you may need specialist help, but often a simple analysis is preferable.

The Structure of the Book

The book is in three parts. The first covers the things you need to get sorted out in advance. The second covers practical aspects of collecting your data. The final part discusses what to do with the data when you have collected them.[*]

In Part I, following the preliminaries discussed in this first chapter:

☐ Chapter 2 tries to help you appreciate some possible approaches to people-focused research and the range of methods you might consider to collect data.
☐ Chapter 3 is concerned with selecting a topic, and getting you to the stage where you have an initial set of research questions; then what overall approach or style of research and method(s) of collecting data will be best fitted to get you answers.

Part II is:

☐ Chapter 4, and covers the practicalities of actually collecting data.

---

[*] Strictly speaking, 'data' are plural – the singular is 'datum'. However, language use changes and it is now often treated as a singular noun. I prefer the plural, but unless your course handbook gives a ruling on which you should use, it's up to you. Be consistent once you have decided.

In Part III:

☐ Chapter 5 focuses on what to do with the data, and
☐ Chapter 6 deals with report writing and other ways of disseminating your findings.

This is, I hope, a logical, and understandable, sequence. However, it may give the mistaken impression that research is a tidy, essentially linear, process where one moves through the various stages and the report pops out at the end. In practice, it is often much more messy and interactive than this. You may find that there are constraints or limitations on what is possible, which crop up at a late stage and force you to change tack. Or, an opportunity to do something different comes out of the blue. Your reading, or discussions with colleagues or a supervisor, or what you get from participants, may make you realize that what you had proposed was wrong-headed. Pilot studies may reveal that you have grossly under-estimated the time things take, etc., etc. (see Chapter 4, p. 97).

Specific 'non-linear' aspects to consider include:

☐ Being prepared to revisit your initial research questions and revise them in the light of the way things are turning out. At one extreme you may find, towards the end, that you have found answers to different questions! Be grateful for such mercies.
☐ Sorting out any arrangements for access as soon as you are reasonably certain of the nature of your project, and of any access needs.
☐ Ensuring that your design is such that you will be able to carry out any analyses you need to do (e.g. that sample sizes are large enough for particular statistical tests to be possible). This means that you need to know how the data will be analysed before they are collected.

It is never too early to start writing. Don't leave it all to the end. Drafts of substantial chunks can be done along the way. Many potentially highquality projects are ruined by a mad scramble to complete the analysis and the report, trying to meet what has become an impossibly tight deadline.

End of Chapter Tasks

Each of the chapters is followed by a set of 'tasks'. These are suggestions about things to do, arising from the material covered in that chapter.

Whether you complete all, or even any of them, is obviously up to you. My recommendation is that you:

☐ *Start the Chapter 1 tasks now*, or at least as soon as practicable.
☐ *Then read through the whole of the book* so that you get a feel for all aspects of completing the project. Don't worry at this stage if you don't follow everything. Note the tasks and by all means give some preliminary thoughts about what you might do, but don't actually complete them.
☐ *Return to the beginning and*, working in 'real time' (i.e. the time dictated by the requirements of the project) *go through the chapter tasks* broadly in sequence, re-reading material in the chapter as necessary. It may make sense to combine tasks for different chapters depending on how things work out.

Further Reading

It's a good idea to start by reading the rest of this book. Do it as rapidly as you can. There are plenty of suggestions for other books to consult as you go through the following chapters.

🕸 *The website (www.wiley.com/college/robson) gives links to general materials useful when thinking about your project*

Chapter 1 Tasks

1 *Get a Project Diary.* This is a notebook in which you enter a variety of things relevant to the project. It can take many different forms but I like to have a nice quality one with hardback covers and not just a loose-leaf writing pad. I suspect that, psychologically, if you have invested in something like this, it gives an added impetus to keeping a quality record. Who knows, it might be the start of your career library of project diaries. An alternative is to have the equivalent of this diary on your computer (make sure you keep back-ups). The kinds of things which might be entered into your diary include:

☐ Notes of all meetings and data collection sessions relating to the project – particularly of meetings with a supervisor. If the data or full notes are somewhere else, give details of where they are.
☐ Appointments made, and kept.
☐ Notes from library, internet and other information gathering sessions.

☐ Memos to yourself about any aspect of the project – what you are proposing to do, and why.

☐ Notes about the modification of earlier intentions and why they are made.

☐ Responses to the later tasks in the book.

☐ Reminders of things to be done, people to be chased up, etc.

☐ Taking stock of where you are; short interim reports of progress, problems and worries, memos to yourself of bright thoughts you have had (get it down before you forget!), suggestions for what might be done.

The diary can be invaluable when you get to the stage of putting together the findings of the project and writing the report. It acts as a memory jogger and an invaluable brake on any tendencies to rewrite history. It is, in itself, a learning tool for future research projects.

2 *Start using it.* In particular it will be useful if you can write down a short account of your initial thoughts about the project you are hoping to do (don't worry if you are not at all sure at this stage – it's what you do by the end that counts). Half a page, or so, is enough. There is a lot to be said in favour of doing this before reading further in the book as it will then be possible for you to look at it later, and gain insights into how far you have travelled in the process of doing the project.

3 *Investigate possibilities for collaboration.* If the idea of carrying out your project on some kind of group basis interests you, then now is the time to find out what may be possible:

☐ Is it allowed? Are there regulations or rules that forbid group work – or particular kinds of group work? Find out.

☐ Are there other students you could work with? If so, get together and sort out what kind of group you can agree on. Get started by sharing ideas on what topic(s) you might go for.

Even if a group project of some kind is not possible, for whatever reason, everyone can benefit from being part of a *support group*. Set one up now.

2

Using Social Research Methods

If you plan to use social research methods, there are some things you need to know about. Planning, developing and delivering a questionnaire of acceptable degree-level standard is not easy without assistance. Researchers over the years have had a great deal of experience in doing this. Build on their experience through reading or discussion and the task becomes feasible for a first-time researcher. The same is true for each and every one of the large number of different social research methods which are now available.

These methods are typically set within well-established traditional approaches to doing research in disciplines such as psychology, sociology and anthropology which are the home bases of the methods. And in fields such as education and health, where their use is well established. Most methodologists (academics specializing in approaches to carrying out research) maintain that an understanding of the theoretical background and in particular, its philosophical underpinning, is also essential for a researcher carrying out a project using social research methods. While many practising and published researchers seem to get on very well without referring to such matters, if the expectation is that your undergraduate research project report should deal with them, that is what you do.

The chapter first covers some general issues, then reviews commonly followed approaches to carrying out social research. It goes on to introduce some of the many methods of data collection which can be used.

A Concern for the Truth

Research, including social research, tries to get at the 'truth'. The scare quotes around 'truth' indicate that philosophers have difficulty deciding what it means – and how we would know when, or if, we had found it. For our purposes, it's best to contrast it with what you should not be doing. You should not be out to 'sell' something. You are not just seeking evidence to push some particular line. Or to support some pet notion or theory.

This can get difficult. You don't stop being a human being when you do research. You are likely to come to any topic with pre-existing views, particularly if you choose something that interests you (which is a very sensible thing to do). Researchers inevitably bring their values and opinions with them when researching. The task is to work at making sure that this doesn't bias the research.

It boils down to working:

☐ *Systematically* – where you have given serious thought to what you are doing and how you are going to do it
☐ *Sceptically* – where you challenge your ideas and findings and get others to do the same (have you really justified what you are claiming, have you considered alternatives?), and
☐ *Ethically* – where you seek to ensure that you are not harming those taking part in the research, or who might be affected by it. And where you don't pass off other people's work as your own, or invent data.

Following these guidelines can, in itself, go a long way toward carrying out a simple project. However, as emphasized above, there is a substantial tradition of ways in which social research has been done, and expertise in the use of the different ways of collecting data, which it makes sense to build on.

Different Purposes of Research

Your personal purpose in choosing a particular topic, your reason for doing so, can be that you have wanted to do so since you started the course, or even before then. Or that it is currently 'hot'. Or it concerns a problem or issue you have recently come across, either in your work or reading, in a journal or wherever. Avoid being pushed into focusing on something which bores you – you are unlikely to do a good project, possibly won't even finish it. Interest in the topic is central. It is what will keep you going when you reach a sticky patch. As you will.

Purpose is commonly thought of by researchers in a rather different way – in terms of what a project seeks to achieve. Some claim that the only acceptable purpose of doing research is to provide explanations. Others think that worthwhile research can focus on describing something, or on conducting an exploration of some little-known phenomenon. In projects involving people, many researchers would maintain that they have a responsibility to seek to improve the lot of those who get a raw deal in society – sometimes referred to as having an emancipatory purpose.

Description

Description is sometimes regarded as too mundane a purpose to qualify as research. Some descriptions are undoubtedly so trivial that they are clearly not worthy of the name. However, a descriptive study carried out with the 'systematically, sceptically, and ethically' hallmarks discussed above, and which provides answers to a well thought through set of research questions, could be of real value.

Exploration

There are, similarly, researchers who look down their noses at an exploratory study. Nothing but a fishing trip! In new and poorly understood areas, exploration could well be the most useful tactic. It is the quality of the work which should determine its research status rather than the purpose.

Explanation

The above arguments for taking a broad church view of research purposes should not be taken as denying the importance of explanatory research. It could reasonably be argued that there is a kind of hierarchy, where description and exploration provide precursors to the task of providing explanations of what is going on in some researched situation.

We have an explanation when we have a good idea about 'what is going on' in the situation we are researching. Perhaps we recognize that it is an example of a particular type of situation, or that some existing theory applies. Or needs modifying, or developing, to account for what we have found.

One way of looking at this which I find helpful is to think in terms of mechanisms. This is common in many fields of research. The mechanism of refraction and reflection of light in water droplets provides a simple explanation of the formation of rainbows. Similarly, Darwin provided a convincing set of mechanisms explaining evolutionary changes. The approach is now being used in social research by those who are concerned that while 'gold standard' randomized control trials can provide strong evidence about the effectiveness or otherwise of some intervention, they give little help in explaining or understanding why the effect takes place. This topic is returned to in discussing the interpretation of research findings (Chapter 5, p. 126).

Emancipation

Here the purpose is to empower oppressed groups (such as women, minorities, or persons with disabilities). This has been a strong theme in much feminist research. It involves a study not only of their lives and experiences, but also of how their oppressors maintain their dominance. One of the complexities of research with an emancipatory purpose is that the (relatively powerful) researcher is called upon to relinquish this power to the (relatively powerless) group.

Research Design

'Design deals primarily with aims, uses, purposes, intentions and plans' (Hakim, 2000; p. 1). She also stresses its concern with practical constraints set by the resources available, and that it is very much about style. She makes an analogy with the role of the architect in building design. Houses erected by builders without benefit of an architect can provide an awful warning. You can build your research project simply by following one or more of the standard research methods. However, by giving thought to the overall design of your project (and of how a particular research method, such as using questionnaires, suits it), you are more likely to end up with something fit for its purpose.

In some disciplines or fields of study, the rule is that an undergraduate project must involve you collecting your own data or information as the central part of the project (sometimes referred to as primary data collection). In others, projects are typically based on collecting secondary data – information that already exists in some form which you study, interpret and analyse and then write about. The latter type are commonly referred to as 'library' or 'desk-bound' projects – though given the increasing reliance on material obtained from the internet accessed via laptops, tablets, etc., these may now be confusing descriptions. Other disciplines or fields of study may permit either type of project. As ever, you must find out what is expected on your course before committing yourself.

If you are free to choose, then your selection should be guided by what you are interested in finding out. In other words, by your research questions. A second consideration is the type of approach and methods of data collection which attract you and which you feel comfortable with. If you find some unattractive, then come up with research questions which call for other approaches and/or research methods. I would run a mile from a project using cold calling by telephone!

There are two very different types of research design commonly used in social research involving primary data collection, which can be characterized as 'fixed' and 'flexible' designs. They are often referred to as 'quantitative' and 'qualitative' designs respectively. However, I think those labels are confusing, as discussed on p. 23.

Flexible designs

With flexible designs you do some preliminary work to sort out the focus of your research and the general approach you will be taking, and perhaps have initial ideas about the research questions to which you will be seeking answers. However, you start the data collection in earnest at a much earlier stage of preparation than in fixed design research. With this style, decisions about how to proceed depend to a considerable extent on what you find out from the early data collection. Hence the design evolves. You might change tack to follow an interesting aspect which has been revealed. Or because your initial plan isn't yielding anything worthwhile. Or you are meeting resistance and find that something is too sensitive. Your research questions will be likely to change and develop as well. Of the approaches mentioned in this chapter, action research, case studies and qualitative research almost always call for this type of design.

Fixed designs

With this style of design, you work out most aspects of the design before carrying out the main collection of data. There may be some preliminary data collection at an early stage to test out ideas and see whether they are practical. Such piloting is indeed highly desirable (see Chapter 4, p. 97). Surveys and experiments are the classic examples of fixed design research.

Qualitative and quantitative data collection

Flexible designs almost always rely heavily on collecting qualitative data, often in the form of words. Fixed designs almost always rely heavily on collecting quantitative data in the form of numbers. Indeed they have in the past been commonly referred to as qualitative and quantitative designs respectively. However, in principle, there is nothing to stop the use of methods yielding qualitative data in fixed designs, or ones yielding quantitative data in flexible designs – there can be considerable advantage in using a mixture of methods in many situations.

Demands on Researchers

The demands on a researcher are rather different when using fixed or flexible designs. Some would find it very difficult to cope with the uncertainties, and need to re-evaluate one's position and possibly make major changes, central to flexible design research. Others will find this an exhilarating challenge. Some would welcome the security and satisfaction of rolling out a well thought through detailed plan. Others want to get involved early on and find the need for extensive pre-planning off-putting.

It is as well to know where you stand on these issues before committing yourself. However, as discussed in the next chapter, p. 63, fixed and flexible designs are best fitted to rather different types of research question. So, as in the choice of whether you collect primary data or do a purely library-based project, there will be constraints on the questions you can target if you don't feel comfortable with the particular demands of one of the styles.

Different Approaches to Doing Social Research

Box 2.1 gives brief details of several general approaches to doing social research methods, together with some of their advantages and disadvantages. Box 2.3 on p. 40 covers a range of commonly used methods of data collection in a similar way. Many degree programmes provide courses in social research methods and methodology, in part to prepare students for final year research projects. The material here will act as a refresher for such students. However, further reading about the different approaches is recommended, particularly if this is new to you.

Box 2.1 Commonly used general approaches

a. Used in Flexible Design Research

	Advantages	Disadvantages
Action research Research aiming to bring about change, and directly involving researchers and participants in the process	1. A collaborative approach giving an active role to participants, hence a more democratic form of research than most approaches. 2. Particularly suitable for practitioner-researchers, contributing to their professional	1. The closely involved, collaborative stance required is difficult for a novice researcher. 2. Access can be difficult for all apart from 'insider' researchers. 3. The shared ownership of the research process between researcher

---

	Advantages	Disadvantages
	and personal development. 3. The effect that the presence of the researcher has on the situation is integral to action research rather than a methodological problem. 4. Provides a means of addressing and resolving practical problems. 5. If successful, can institute a continuing cycle of development and change in an organization.	and participant can lead to problems, particularly in completion of the project to time. 4. Active cooperation by participants is essential, but is difficult to achieve as it takes place in the work setting where there can be conflicting demands. 5. The non-traditional researcher role called for, with its inevitable loss in detachment and impartiality, may not be acceptable in some course regulations.
Case study Research focusing on a single case, or a small number of cases. The case can be a person, institution, situation or whatever.	1. Studying a single case (or a small number of cases) gives the opportunity to carry out a study in depth, which can capture complexities, relationships and processes. 2. It strongly encourages the use	1. The credibility of generalizations from case studies is often challenged. It depends on a different logic from that familiar in surveys. 2. Case studies typically seek to focus on situations as they occur naturally and

	Advantages	Disadvantages
	of multiple methods of collecting data and of multiple data sources. 3. The boundaries of the study (e.g. the amount of time involved and context covered), are flexible and can often be tailored to the time and resources you have available. 4. It is less artificial and detached than traditional approaches such as experiments and surveys. 5. Can be used for a wide variety of research purposes, and for widely different types of cases.	hence observer effects caused by the presence of the researcher can be problematic. 3. You have to be prepared to modify your approach, depending on the results of your involvement. It can become difficult to keep to deadlines. 4. The continuing, though erroneous, view that case study is necessarily a 'soft option', may lead to it not being acceptable in some course regulations.
Ethnographic approach Research focusing on the description and understanding of the life and customs of people living in a specific culture.	1. Ethnographic style studies (as distinct from so-called 'full ethnographies') are feasible within the constraints of time and resources of undergraduate projects. 2. Relies largely upon direct, usually	1. Can be very difficult and confusing for the novice researcher to come to terms with their participant observer role (tensions between being a participant and an observer).

	Advantages	Disadvantages
	participant, observation and does not call for other specialized data collection methods. 3. Particularly suitable for studies focusing on how members of a culture see events. 4. Results in rich data focusing on processes and relationships set in context. 5. Can be very involving and interesting.	2. The skills needed to understand what is going on in a strange situation, including decisions on the choice of informants, may need considerable experience to acquire. Practitioner-researchers working in familiar settings have the converse problem of 'making the familiar strange' (i.e. needing to set aside their preconceptions). 3. Ethnography traditionally seeks to move from the purely descriptive to provide theoretical explanations, which is not an easy task. 4. Ethical issues abound, including the avoidance of deception (e.g. about one's role), obtaining informed consent, and intrusions on privacy.

	Advantages	Disadvantages
		5. Access can be difficult to obtain. 6. Similar problems of generalizability of findings to those with case studies.
Grounded theory approach Focuses on the systematic discovery of theory from data so that the theories are grounded in observations of the social world.	1. Widely used as a method for generating or deriving theory from a research project (usually, but not necessarily, qualitative). 2. Provides useful prescriptions for the process of carrying out flexible design projects. 3. Provides a detailed set of rules and procedures for the coding and analysis of qualitative data.	1. The very specific terminology and highly prescriptive coding rules have acquired something of a cult status (however it is possible to adopt the general style of the approach without buying in to all of this). 2. Strict insistence that the theory must be generated from the data collected ignores what researchers bring to the analysis from their previous experience and reading. 3. There are different variants of grounded theory now put forward by its founders.

General qualitative approaches
Some researchers who design projects involving collecting qualitative data, simply refer to their work as 'Qualitative'. Others follow very specific named approaches.

b. Used in Fixed Design Research

	Advantages	Disadvantages
Experimental approach Depends on the researcher actively manipulating or changing aspects of what is studied. Typically involves allocating or assigning participants to different experimental conditions.	1. Provides the possibility of getting clear and unambiguous answers to very specific research questions. 2. The very tight specification of the conditions of the laboratory experiment permits replication and hence the checking of findings. 3. Laboratory experiments eliminate the problem of gaining access. You don't have to spend time and resources travelling to and from the site of the research. 4. Regarded traditionally as the method of choice for demonstrating causal relationships.	1. Experiments are not feasible unless there is extensive prior knowledge about the topic. 2. It is difficult to avoid artificiality, particularly in laboratory experiments, making the application of findings to real world issues problematic. 3. The control by the experimenter of relevant variables central to experimentation can raise difficult ethical problems. 4. This control can be difficult to achieve in field experiments. 5. Finding a statistically significant result does not, in itself, help to explain why the result was obtained.

	Advantages	Disadvantages
Surveys Involves collecting data from groups of participants on a range of variables typically using questionnaires.	1. A very widely used approach whose results communicate well with many different audiences. 2. Typically produces quantitative data which can be easily subjected to statistical analysis, using straightforward computer-based techniques. 3. It is possible to predict relatively accurately the amount of time and resources needed to complete data collection and analysis. 4. Large sample sizes can be sought without major cost implications (if a questionnaire is used the major proportion of the cost is associated with its design). 5. Use of representative samples from known populations leads to readily	1. There can be misplaced confidence in the findings, particularly when there are deficiencies in sampling or response rates are relatively low. 2. It is increasingly difficult to achieve acceptable response rates from the widely used postal survey. 3. There is typically little or no check on the seriousness or honesty with which respondents approach the task of completing a survey. 4. Surveys usually lack detail and depth, as lengthy and complex questionnaires will affect response rates. 5. Surveys do not permit exploration of the context of the phenomenon studied.

	Advantages	Disadvantages
	generalizable results, where the situation in the population can be estimated with known probability.	

c. Used in Fixed or Flexible Design Research

	Advantages	Disadvantages
Evaluation research Research focusing on assessing the worth or value of some intervention or approach. A wide variety of designs can be used.	1. It provides a research tool for addressing the accountability now called for in almost all areas of society. 2. There are many different types of evaluation suitable for different research questions. 3. Sensitively handled, evaluations have an important role in improving services and the functioning of organizations.	1. They should be approached with care by novice researchers owing to the almost inevitable sensitivity of an evaluative study. 2. Ethical issues abound, particularly concerning evaluations which may result in harm to any of those involved. 3. Access is problematic. Even when formal access is granted, there can be internal resistance and obstruction.

> 🏛 *The website (www.wiley.com/college/robson) provides suggestions for further reading on the different approaches*

The advantage of working within the established research traditions covered in Box 2.1 is that many of the problems and pitfalls have already been thought through. There are agreed ways of doing things which gives reassurance. If you are brave (foolhardy?) you may want to strike out on your own and not follow one of these well-trodden paths. In practice, whatever you do is almost inevitably going to have features of one or more existing research traditions. So you may as well capitalize on the experience of others.

'Library' studies

The approaches discussed in the previous section all involve you collecting some new data for your project. This is a required feature of many undergraduate research projects. Using some existing or 'secondary' data as well as collecting new 'primary' data will not be a problem. However, some regulations permit, or expect, students to work exclusively with secondary data. If you are considering doing this, check your degree regulations.

The traditional label has been a 'library' study but the vast resources now available from the internet mean that you need not actually visit a library to get almost any type of existing data. A project based on existing data could be effectively an expanded literature review. However, it is likely that the key sources that you are using will need to be subjected to a detailed and exhaustive analysis where the techniques of 'documentary analysis', covered below as a method of collecting data, can be used.

Examples from Undergraduate Projects

Recent years have seen a large increase in the number of journals which focus on articles based on research carried out by undergraduates. Box 2.2 provides summaries of examples using the various approaches covered in Box 2.1. They illustrate the wide variety of topics chosen and give some indication of what is feasible as an undergraduate project or dissertation. Full references for the articles are in the Author Index at the end of the book.

Methods of Collecting Data

Box 2.3 lists a range of commonly used data collecting methods and their advantages and disadvantages.

Box 2.2 Examples from undergraduate projects using different approaches

a. Flexible Designs

1. Action research approach

Fluency and fun in Spanish through TPRS: An action research project. Angela Armstrong took this approach because she wanted to improve her own teaching and hence the learning of her students. As is typical of action research, the project involved various cycles of activity where she used TPRS (Total Physical Response Storytelling) to teach Spanish through stories, dramatic play and body movements and collected data to assess the learning and enjoyment of school students (Armstrong, 2008).

Combating the privatisation of life in a neo-liberal regime: The fight for water democracies. Gavin Raders used participatory action research in a study which also involved an ethnographic approach and documentary analysis as part of Indian farmers' successful attempts to close down a large Coca Cola bottling plant (Raders, 2008).

How the sport education model supports the inclusion of children marginalised as lower ability in physical education. Stephanie McDonnell used a participatory action research approach involving a combination of observation and interviews as well as a class teacher's reflective evaluation to investigate how an SE (Sport Education) model can support the active participation of children with low motor skills and low confidence in physical education (McDonnell, 2011).

2. Case study approach

Swaziland: A protective environment for children? Utilising and evaluating the UNICEF framework in a developing society. Lydia Marshall carried out an ethnographic case study in Lobamba, Swaziland. Her aim was both to investigate to what extent Swaziland is a protective environment for children according to this framework and to consider whether the model needs reassessing in the light of the different economic, social and cultural values of a developing southern African country. She also focused on the positive roles which children in Swaziland play in the lives of their families and communities (Marshall, 2009).

Image reparation strategies in sports: Media analysis of Kobe Bryant and Barry Bonds. Jennifer Kennedy's project involved case studies of two scandals in the US professional sports world. By examining media coverage of the two athletes during the scandals, she studied the effectiveness of different image reparation strategies and suggests guidelines to follow in establishing and maintaining an athlete's positive image throughout a scandal (Kennedy, 2010).

The impacts of educational attainment, professional interests and residency on community involvement and civic engagement. Elizabeth Young carried out a case study of civically engaged individuals in a specific suburban locality and compared them with Census data and Community Population Survey data to evaluate the specific sample group within the locality in comparison to the broader population of the locality and the national population (Young, 2011).

3. Ethnographic approach

'Linguistic habitus' and the domination of Latino workers in the American restaurant industry: An ethnographic sketch. Eric Thornton argued that the US restaurant industry as we know it could not exist without the labour of Latin American immigrants. And that these workers do not enjoy a financial return and recognition equal to that of their 'native' counterparts. Through work-time participant observation and interviews with New York restaurant professionals, he revealed a pattern of social domination existing along the lines of immigrant status that is endemic to the restaurant industry and upon which that industry and its culture depend (Thornton, 2011).

The educational experiences of gypsy travellers: The impact of cultural dissonance. Danny Wilding's study sought to discover if there was any evidence of conflict in the educational experiences of gypsy travellers in an English middle school. Through the adoption of the role of 'observer as participant' and the use of semi-structured interviews, the study sought to place the experiences and the voices of the gypsy travellers at the centre of the research. From the results it was evident that conflict of various forms, but most often that of a subtle nature, was an everyday feature of their educational experiences at the school (Wilding, 2008).

Community gardens or gardening communities: A survey of community gardens on Austin's East Side. Ania Upstill collected qualitative data on the use of community gardens on the East Side of Austin, Texas. She chose to do a multi-sited ethnographic study based on interviews with garden coordinators augmented by participant observation. In order to gather additional information, she also attended garden workdays and conducted a spatial analysis of the gardens within the surrounding neighbourhoods. She discusses reasons why the community gardens are being used by newer, more privileged residents rather than the disadvantaged residents who stand to gain more from them (Upstill, 2011).

4. Grounded theory

Sister sister: Interpreting intimacy in sibling relationships. Whitney Stach explored what constitutes intimacy in sister relationships and how this is communicated. She interviewed females with sisters using a semi-structured interview approach. Data were analysed following Strauss and Corbin's grounded theory method. Her conclusions were that sisters share a unique relationship, using it to develop as an individual which is important to the relationship, and that the intimate nature is highly reliant on their upbringing and family life (Stach, 2007).

Creating Patagonia national park: Understanding community response to national park creation by a private foreign non-profit organization. Elena Bantle used a combination of archival research, participant observation, informal conversation with involved parties, and semi-structured interviews to examine the nature of the relationship between foreign, private, non-profit representatives and former users of the landscape in national park creation and administration at Patagonia National Park. Through grounded theory analysis of the data and integration of previous research, she suggests a model for understanding community response to this form of park creation (Bantle, 2010).

Message communication in advertising: Selling the Abercrombie and Fitch image. Claire Driessen carried out a qualitative content analysis of Abercrombie and Fitch's new campaign, uncovered the messages sent to consumers and how those messages were packaged. She employed Strauss and Corbin's approach to data analysis. The emergent messages from the campaign are discussed (Driessen, 2005).

5. General qualitative research approach

The development of religious tolerance: Co-operative board games with children and adolescents. Minna Lehtonen explored how developmental differences in religious identity are linked to tolerance and attempted to identify developmental differences in the ways children demonstrate tolerance in social interactions. A religion-themed collaborative board game designed for the study was played by small groups of children from primary and secondary schools who were observed and audio recorded. Transcripts of the conversations were analysed using qualitative content analysis and conversational analysis. A reluctance to disagree and challenge others in the younger sample contrasted with more direct disagreements and compromises among the adolescents (Lehtonen, 2009).

Encouraging female entrepreneurship: Lessons from Colombian women. Jennifer Quigley-Jones interviewed twelve Colombian female entrepreneurs using a questionnaire covering their motivations, media presentation of female entrepreneurs, government restrictions, investment opportunities, female business networks, and the confidence of female entrepreneurs. Interviewees were selected to reflect the diversity within Colombian female entrepreneurship and transcripts analysed qualitatively. Reasons for the relatively small entrepreneurial gender gap in Colombia compared to UK were explored (Quigley-Jones, 2012).

Donor insemination: The role of the internet in the experiences of donor offspring, DI parents and donors. Alison Wheatley's study aimed to discover the ways in which the internet was used to negotiate the issues surrounding donor insemination, including its role in providing a support network and as a tool with which to establish contact with donors and other kin. The study used e-mail for semi-structured interviews to investigate the ways in which groups interacted with each other and how those interactions shaped their choices. The qualitative data were analysed using thematic coding. She concluded that the internet is very important in providing both a community network for support, advice and validation and a tool for negotiating kinship (Wheatley, 2010).

b. Fixed Designs

1. Survey approach

Online social networking and e-safety: Analysis of risk-taking behaviours and negative online experiences among adolescents. In recent years the internet has become a pivotal resource in the lives of many adolescents and young adults. However, its use has attracted a wealth of media attention focusing on the risks and potential negative consequences of using such online tools. In a project by Paul McGivern and Nathalie Noret, 638 adolescents completed an online survey exploring school experiences and use of the internet. The key findings indicate that, while incidents such as cyber bullying and cyber stalking do frequently occur among adolescents, their prevalence may not be as extreme as portrayed by the media or as perceived by the general public (McGivern & Noret, 2011).

Childhood obesity: The role of dairy products. Jennifer Harguth's project had two aspects. Children took a survey questionnaire home for completion by their parents. Demographics were included on the survey in order to calculate the body mass index (BMI). Other questions involved whether the students eat breakfast at home or at school, or if they rarely eat breakfast. Lunch beverage choices were analysed as well as a typical after-school snack. In a second aspect children were invited to choose a beverage at a booth in a grocery store from a carbonated soft drink (Mountain Dew), chocolate milk, white milk, apple juice, orange juice and water. Data were gathered on the children's gender, age, choice, and whether or not the parent/guardian held an influence in the decision making. Information on the parent's preference was also recorded for analysis (Harguth, 2010).

A nutrition assessment of dietary practices of Mexicans living in the state of Veracruz, Mexico. In an effort to identify the traditional foods that make up the Mexican diet, Melissa Barth travelled through the state of Veracruz, Mexico and compiled data describing the types of foods eaten and the frequency of their consumption. 453 questionnaires were collected in three communities. Slight differences in food consumption patterns emerged between different age groups and communities, but the core foods that make up the traditional Mexican diet were still able to be determined. This core diet could then be compared to the adapted core diet of Mexican Americans. With adequate and appropriate food substitutions taking place, the Mexican American consumer can maintain a healthy and relatively traditional diet while living in a new culture (Barth, 2008).

2. Experimental approach

The criminal face effect: Physical attractiveness and character integrity as determinants of perceived criminality. Alex Hodgkiss and Claire Handy showed participants attractive and unattractive portraits paired with a positive, negative or no-character statement in a repeated measures experimental design. A 2 x 3 factorial analysis of variance showed main effects of attractiveness and character on crime rating. However, a predicted interaction between the variables was not significant and some of the results were inconsistent (Hodgkiss & Handy, 2007).

Do you want the good news or the bad news first? News order influences recipients' mood, perceptions, and behaviors. Ann Nguyen examined whether news order has affective, cognitive, and behavioural consequences. Participants completed a personality test and received fake results in either a 'good then bad,' 'bad then good,' or 'bad only' order. They completed questionnaires about how they felt about their results and chose whether to watch a personality improvement video. Results revealed that news order has consequences. People who received good news last reported better mood and appraisal of the results. Additionally, people who received bad news last reported greater intentions for behavioural change and were more likely to watch the improvement video (Nguyen, 2011).

Attitudes toward persons with disabilities: A comparison of Chinese and American students. Molly Grames and Cortney Leverentz compared the attitudes of American college students to those of Chinese international college students in the United States. Participants completed the Attitudes Toward Persons with Disabilities Scale and a Q-sort by ranking nine cards describing individuals with varying disability types and severities according to preference. Significant differences were found among the three disability types. The Chinese students reported more favorable attitudes toward persons with disabilities (Grames & Leverentz, 2010).

c. Fixed or Flexible

Evaluation research

Using knowledge interventions to determine stress and future preventative behaviour regarding cervical cancer and the human papilloma virus. Clare Austin obtained ethical consent to use an experimental design to evaluate the effectiveness of providing information about the human papilloma virus, cervical cancer and cervical screening. All participants received a baseline questionnaire assessing their current lifestyle and knowledge about the topic. These measures were repeated after the knowledge intervention. Participants were randomly assigned to an intervention group or a non-intervention group where they received the same knowledge questions about the human papilloma virus, cervical cancer and cervical screening via the knowledge intervention. However, those in the intervention group received the correct answers to each question after submitting their answer along with further information, whereas those in the non-intervention group did not until after the study was completed and they were debriefed. There were few statistical differences in knowledge between the groups post-intervention. However, there were indications that the knowledge intervention heightened participants' stress regarding the virus (Austin, 2010).

Fighting the addiction: The effectiveness of the La Crosse County drug court program. Erin Petrus developed a questionnaire on illegal drug use prior to the drug court program and current illegal drug use, as well as legal drug use before and after. Questions regarding reasons for using and stopping using drugs were also asked, along with other questions such as length since completion of the program and number of relapses. The data provided useful information on ways to work with participants during the program in order to reduce their risk of relapse while in the program (Petrus, 2007).

An evaluation of physical impacts in backcountry camping areas at Glacier national park. Rachel Tadt evaluated three backcountry campgrounds using a range of different indices and observations. These included ratings of facilities, their impact on the environment, counts of unofficial trails and tree damage. She also rated both the campground sites and the facilities, to determine any major deficiencies in the facilities and areas of obvious non-compliance with campground design standards. Unofficial human caused trails, tree damage, illegal fire sites, amount of litter and number of waste sites were all assessed. On completion, she interviewed the wilderness manager of the Park to discuss the resource management methods used and how to maximize the potential use of the wilderness with the least amount of impact on park resources (Tadt, 2007).

d. Library Studies

The construction of 'peoplehood' in the second wave of Norwegian black metal. Owen Fung focused exclusively on the construction of 'Norwegian people' in the music, artwork, writings and interviews associated with the second-wave Norwegian black metal scene. Based on music, artwork, interviews and writings by musicians, the analysis demonstrates how different discourses are deployed to engender a specific representation of 'Norwegian peoplehood'. The reliance on second-hand interview data poses certain limitations on the argument made. However, within the bounds of available resources, an empirical study was not feasible (Fung, 2010).

Entitled to benefit? A review of state benefit take up by older people belonging to black and minority ethnic groups. Eleanor Scharf drew on evidence from research which explores the experiences of older people from black and minority ethnic (BME) groups living in the UK. She also gathered information from reports by stakeholder organizations and agencies on the experiences of BME older people, including Age Concern, Help the Aged and the Policy Research Institute on Ageing and Ethnicity. These sources are supported by a range of statistical data that reflect the UK's growing diversity with regard to age and ethnicity. After outlining the types of barriers experienced in accessing their benefit entitlements, she proposes a number of ways in which under-claiming may be challenged and overcome (Scharf, 2010).

The National Association of Professional Base Ball Players: The origins of professional baseball and the American identity. Eric Rosenberg analysed the development of the sport of baseball into a professional industry alongside the concurrent industrialization and urbanization of the United States using primary documents from the era as well as modern historians' accounts of early baseball. He also relied on sources focusing on the changing American identity during this period and concludes that baseball's progression into a professional league from grassroots origins compared to a broader trend of the ideal American being viewed as urban, skilled, and affluent. His analysis of the National Association of Professional Base Ball Players provides insight on the formative experience of the modern collective American identity and baseball's place in it (Rosenberg, 2012).

Box 2.3 Methods of collecting data

	Advantages	Disadvantages
Interviews	1. It's a research version of something you do all the time – talking to people. Provided you like talking to people (often strangers), it can be enjoyable. 2. There is usually relatively little resistance to being interviewed (by comparison with other methods, such as asking participants to complete questionnaires). Hence, there is rarely a problem in achieving high response rates.	1. It can be difficult to keep 'on topic', especially if you are both enjoying the interview. 2. Can take up a lot of time, particularly if you have to travel (consider telephone interviews if this is a problem). 3. You need good social skills to interview well. 4. They either require much preparation and piloting (with more structured interviews) or call for well-developed research

	Advantages	Disadvantages
	3. No special equipment is needed apart from a good voice recorder and microphone. 4. The face-to-face situation gives you the opportunity to develop empathy with the interviewee, which can help in getting better, fuller, responses, and increase the chance that they will take the questions seriously. 5. This also gives you the chance of assessing the value of their answers, through non-verbals, throw-away comments, etc. 6. There are different types of interview, so you can select a style appropriate for many different approaches to research including both fixed and flexible designs.	skills and experience (with less structured interviews). 5. Apart from highly structured interviews (where the analysis is usually straightforward), they usually need to be recorded, followed by lengthy transcription and analysis. 6. They are subject to bias (e.g. interviewees are likely to say what they think you want to hear, or which puts them in a good light).
Questionnaires	1. It is possible to deal with a large sample even if you have relatively small resources (applies particularly to postal questionnaires).	1. It can be very difficult to obtain acceptably high response rates. Efforts to improve response rates can involve substantial additional time and resources.

	Advantages	Disadvantages
	2. The use of pre-coded answers simplifies the task of analysis. 3. They do not require personal interaction skills on the part of the researcher. 4. Absence of face-to-face interaction between researcher and participants reduces the effect of the researcher on responses. 5. Can be used via the internet in e-mail or web-based versions.	2. It is not possible to go into topics in depth, as long and complex questionnaires reduce response rates. 3. There is no easy way to check the truthfulness of answers, nor to assess the seriousness with which participants have approached the task. 4. A good questionnaire calls for careful planning and design, and meticulous attention to detail at all phases of the research. 5. The resulting quantitative data and associated statistical analysis can give an inflated impression of the value of the findings.
Tests and scales	1. They can be used to measure many different 'people' things, including attitudes, views, abilities, opinions, etc. 2. They are usually easy to administer, producing a numerical scale value on which people can be compared.	1. Devising a new test for research purposes is complex and time-consuming. 2. Existing tests will often not be exactly right for your purposes. 3. Many of the best tests have restricted availability (i.e. they can only be used by those with particular

	Advantages	Disadvantages
	3. There is a wide range of existing tests which can be picked 'off the shelf', many of which have been developed by experts in the field. 4. Can be used via the internet in e-mail or web-based versions.	professional qualifications). 3. 'Test-aversion' is increasingly common in some groups. 4. Some tests may be viewed as threatening or sensitive, raising strong ethical issues and also affecting their acceptability.
Structured observation	1. Can be used to observe and analyse a very wide range of situations. 2. Provides a record of what people actually do, rather than what they say that they do (as in interviews and questionnaires). 3. Wide range of existing structured observation schedules which can be picked 'off the shelf'. 4. If you can find an existing schedule appropriate for your research, you can generate quantitative data of known reliability and validity. 5. Produces coded quantitative data which can be quickly and easily analysed. 6. The use of very clearly defined observational	1. Devising your own observation schedule is complex and time-consuming. 2. Existing observation schedules will often not be exactly right for your purposes. 3. Even if you find the 'right' schedule, it will take time and effort to be proficient in its use. 4. You need to demonstrate that you have achieved acceptably high standards of reliability in its use, usually through having a colleague provide independent observations. 5. Reactivity (the effects of the observer on what is happening) can be a serious problem.

	Advantages	Disadvantages
	categories reduces the subjectivity and bias found in unstructured observation.	6. Oversimplifies and decontextualizes complex situations, as only a small number of easily observable behaviours can be captured in observation schedules.
Participant observation	1. Can be used to observe and analyse a very wide range of situations. 2. There is little or no need for equipment or prior preparation. 3. Provides the possibility of adopting a wide range of different participant roles (ranging from full participant through to marginal participant) depending on what is appropriate for the research, and which you feel most comfortable with. 4. It is capable of generating rich qualitative data. It is claimed that participant observation provides an opportunity to understand complex realities and relationships.	1. Can be very time-consuming and emotionally demanding. 2. There can be a problem finding opportunities to record what you have observed while it is fresh in your mind, 3. Danger of 'going native'; with your research role being prejudiced by your involvement with the group and its values. 4. Can be hazardous for the researcher. Not only in terms of physical safety, but in being exposed to psychological and possibly legal risks, as well as ethical dilemmas. 5. The data can be overwhelming in both quantity and richness, hence difficult to analyse and interpret.

	Advantages	Disadvantages
	5. Extended involvement in a setting is likely to reduce any effects that the researcher might have on the situation.	
Documentary analysis	1. It is usually not difficult to get hold of relevant documents for little or no cost, when you have access to the facilities of an academic library. 2. Typically a cheap (in resource terms) means of generating substantial amounts of data. 3. Amenable to a wide variety of qualitative and quantitative styles of analysis. 4. Documents are usually in a permanent form and can be returned to for re-analysis, or for the purposes of reliability checking. 5. Provides a potential subsidiary data collection method for almost all projects.	1. As the document has been produced for a purpose other than for your research, you need to assess the extent to which this purpose is likely to affect the document. 2. Assessing the credibility of a document can be complex and difficult. Its authenticity or genuineness has to be established. As well as purpose, aspects such as the position, background, likely biases and prejudices of the author(s) have to be considered. 3. In contrast to the directness of observation, data from documentary analysis are at least two removes from reality. They are based on both the author(s) interpretation and on your own interpretation of this.

	Advantages	Disadvantages
Internet-based research methods	Questionnaires are common in e-mail and web-based surveys, but most of the methods covered above can be adapted for use on the internet.	Their use can raise novel ethical issues which need detailed review.

The website (www.wiley.com/college/robson) provides suggestions for further reading on the different methods of collecting data

Examples from Undergraduate Projects

Box 2.4 provides summaries of examples using the various methods of collecting data covered in Box 2.3. As with the examples of different approaches in Box 2.2, they illustrate the wide variety of topics chosen and give some indication of what is feasible as an undergraduate project or dissertation. Full references for the articles are in the Author Index at the end of the book.

Box 2.4 Examples from undergraduate projects using different methods of collecting data

1. Interviews

The meanings of well-being and intuition in crystal therapy: A qualitative interview study. Fleur Dewsnap sought to provide an insight into the meanings associated with crystals in the world of crystal therapy. She analysed semi-structured interviews with a purposive sample of seven women with experiences of crystal therapy, two of whom were 'therapists'. The findings add to previous work on this topic by emphasizing that respondents in this study utilized the notion of 'well-being', and that while there was a common belief that crystals were capable of influencing other objects or events, there was, nevertheless, some evidence of ambivalence or scepticism about causality. The importance of intuition as a form of knowledge associated with crystal therapy is stressed (Dewsnap & Smart, 2011).

The relationship between unemployment and communist-era legacies in Leipzig, Germany. David Hunn explored the combination of communist legacies and post-communist economic policies that drive the disproportionately high rates of long-term unemployment in Leipzig. He uses the opinions gathered through in-depth interviews with individuals linked to unemployment in different ways, ranging from unemployed people themselves to business development officers. He concludes that the main reason for high unemployment is that the legacies of the German Democratic Republic have created serious socio-economic problems (Hunn, 2009).

Teen and adult activities onboard a cruise ship. Alexandra Goodman was interested in the consumer's viewpoint of teen and adult activities in a commercial recreation setting such as a cruise ship. Her project was based on collecting data on a seven night cruise through the Mediterranean. An onboard survey was used to set up focus group interviews. She also used observation and participation in onboard activities. The results indicate that there are major differences in the number and types of onboard activities favoured by teens and adults (Goodman, 2009).

2. Questionnaires

What's in a voice? Vocal characteristics and their influence on courtroom decision making. Tiffany Entringer and Lee Starck investigated the perceptions of vocal characteristics and their impact on courtroom decision making. Pitch and speech rate were examined for their effects on perceived veracity (truthfulness) of a defendant. An actor recorded a testimony from a hit and run case. A computer program was used to cross-manipulate the levels of pitch and tempo. Participants were randomly assigned to one of nine conditions and presented with the defendant's vocal testimony. It was predicted that lower pitch, and faster rates of speech will be perceived as more truthful, thus less guilty. Responses to a questionnaire did not support the predictions (Entringer & Starck, 2010).

The unravelling of apparel: Online shopping behaviour. Marjolein Kramer sought to obtain a better understanding in the determinants of online shopping for clothing and the interaction between consumers' use of the internet for information search and their choice of channel (i.e. bricks-and-mortar stores or the internet) for their final purchase. Questionnaires were distributed to over 200 students and the data analysed. No interaction was found between in-store shopping for clothing and e-shopping or internet search. Opinions of friends and family turned out to be twice as important for men than for women. Results showed that the Fishbein's Theory of Reasoned Action model helped explain e-shopping for clothing with a few alterations (Kramer, 2012).

Investigation of Wisconsin's family care policy: Research and recommendations concerning employment outcomes for people with disabilities. A new long-term care system for people with developmental and physical disabilities and the elderly, called Family Care, is being implemented in Wisconsin. It allows for care management organizations to provide services related to vocational acquisition and retention for individuals with disabilities. The purpose of Matthew Pesko's study was, first, to explore the relationship between employer outreach efforts, employer attitudes and employment outcomes; and, secondly, to understand the differences, if any, between Wisconsin counties using the Family Care model and counties using the traditional model. A questionnaire-based mail survey, to which 101 care managers and employers responded, measured perceptions of the level of employer outreach, attitudes of area employers and hiring rates for people with disabilities in their counties. Results indicate that disability employment professionals and employers regard the current integrated employment status as neither completely closed-off nor readily conducive for acquisition, but rather somewhere in the middle (Pesko, 2009).

3. Tests and Scales

How an early caregiving style affects adult romantic love. Lisa Dale investigated the theory that adult romantic attachment is reflective of a person's perception of an early caregiving style. She used two existing instruments – Griffin and Bartholomew's scale to measure adult attachment and Hazan and Shaver's parental/caregiving questionnaire to measure perceptions of an early caregiving style. 68 male and female participants from diverse socioeconomic backgrounds participated in the study. The hypothesis was accepted: the warmth of the caregiver was positively correlated to a high secure adult attachment score. A high insecure caregiver score was positively correlated with a high insecure adult attachment score (Dale, 2013).

Judging a book by its album cover: A study of the relationship between musical preference and personality. Louis Dalrymple investigated the relationship between musical preference and personality among first-year undergraduates at his university. A modified version of the Ten Item Personality

Inventory (TIPI) was used to measure personality and the Short Test of Musical Preference (STOMP) to measure musical preference. By collecting, analysing, and comparing data from 20 first-year undergraduates, correlations between specific personality and musical preference dimensions were calculated. The strength and nature of these correlations proved to be in general agreement with prior research. There was no statistically significant difference in these relationships between male and female participants (Dalrymple, 2009).

A comparison of academic stress among Australian and international students. Rachel DeDeyn looked at the differences between the levels of academic stress in Australian and international students living in an international dorm in Melbourne, Australia. 85 students from 21 countries were surveyed using Gadzella's Student-Life Stress Inventory. The results indicated that overall there was no significant difference between the amount of academic stress experienced by Australian students and the amount of academic stress experienced by international students. There was a significant difference found in the subcategory of pressure related stress between Australian and international students. International students reported experiencing less pressure related stress than Australian students (DeDeyn, 2008).

4 a. Structured Observation

Validation of the ActivPAL Activity Monitor as a measure of walking at pre-determined slow walking speeds in a healthy population in a controlled setting. Nadia Kanoun's study aimed to evaluate the criterion-related validity of the activPAL^{TM} activity monitor to measure steps taken when walking at the slow speeds characteristic of elderly and patient populations. A convenience sample of 42 healthy individuals was recruited from a population of students. Validity of the monitor, measuring total steps taken, was compared to direct observation of steps taken using a hand-tally counter during a five minute period of treadmill walking. The results suggest that activPAL^{TM} is a valid measure of steps taken when walking at all but the slowest speed (0.45 metres per second) and hence that it could potentially be used to measure physical activity in populations who walk slowly. However, further investigation of its validity at 0.45 metres per second and in elderly and patient populations is needed (Kanoun, 2009).

Compartmentalization and poor marital outcomes: Are negative conflict resolution tactics to blame? Nadia Velasquez studied whether intimates integrate or segregate positive and negative partner information has important implications for future relationship well-being. In a longitudinal study of newlywed couples (n = 84) she found that greater compartmentalization at the beginning of the marriage predicted lower marital satisfaction two years later. The study included use of a structured observation schedule to assess spouses' communications when discussing a conflict with their partner. Videotaped interactions were divided into two-minute segments for coding and analysed with Sillars Verbal Tactics Coding Scheme (Velasquez, 2012).

Easily frustrated infants: Implications for emotion regulation strategies and cognitive functioning. Nikita Rodrigues used observational sessions in the laboratory to code the behaviour of infants during a frustration task in which they were denied an attractive toy. She identified easily frustrated (n = 9) and less easily frustrated (n = 15) infants from a cohort (n = 54) of 10-month-olds with and without a family history of ADHD on the basis of measures of distress on the frustration task and maternal reports. Easily frustrated infants showed no significant relationship to having a family history of ADHD, but did show differences in frequency of emotion regulation strategies and on assessments of cognitive functioning (Rodrigues, 2012).

4b. Participant Observation

'Linguistic habitus' and the domination of Latino workers in the American restaurant industry: An ethnographic sketch. Eric Thornton's research was almost exclusively focused on the so-called front-of-house service settings in restaurants rather than in the kitchen. He chose to limit the research to dining rooms and taverns as these areas are a more clear-cut expression of the service society. Data were collected primarily by way of work-time participant observation. That is, the data consisted of content from workplace interactions, the interactions which comprise normal daily social life in restaurants. They reveal a pattern of social domination existing along the lines of immigrant status that is endemic to the restaurant industry and upon which that industry and its culture profoundly depend. Utilizing Pierre Bourdieu's social theory, he examines the symbolic means by which this type of domination is legitimized (Thornton, 2011).

Community and exclusion in the gay Mecca. Andrew Levine-Murray was interested in the ways in which marginalization of certain types of people occurs even within public spaces delineated for already marginalized groups. He examined how low-income queer people of colour navigate and negotiate queer urban enclaves, such as the Castro in San Francisco, that present themselves as open to all but are predominantly populated by white middle class men. During weekdays, he volunteered at a community organization and observed daily happenings of the Castro community. On weekend nights he hung out on the corner of Market and Castro Streets, eventually immersing himself in the group of low-income queer people of colour who consistently congregate there. He also conducted in-depth interviews with them, asking about their experiences in the Castro and in their home neighbourhoods, and exploring their re-imaginations of the Castro as a more ideal place (Levine-Murray, 2012).

A study of sexist attitudes among students. Zoe Farr sought to reveal the impact and prevalence of modern sexist attitudes, based on the sexist attitudes of students studied at a university campus. A covert ethnography is used to observe students in different surroundings around the campus at the University of Essex, studying their language and interactions with members of the same and opposite sex, to identify any underlying sexist opinions. The study is based on direct observation in a range of campus settings and is participant only in the sense that she is a student at the university. She uncovered examples of sexism from both males and females, but found that whilst sexism against women was generally considered distasteful (although was discussed with amusement between groups of males on many occasions), sexism against men was received with little or no contention (Farr, 2012).

5. Documentary Analysis

An evaluation of routine screening, assessment and treatment of depression for patients on the diabetes and/or coronary heart disease registers in a primary care practice in Norfolk. Anna Marie Croxford investigated if depression screening in patients with diabetes and/or coronary heart disease (CHD) is performed in accordance with official guidelines, and whether screening leads to the identification and treatment of new depression cases. She carried out a retrospective audit of eligible patients on the diabetes and/or CHD registers at a rural general practice for 12 months and calculated the percentages of patients screened, identified to have depression and subsequently treated. Her conclusions were that current screening at this practice appears unnecessary or unsuccessful (Croxford, 2010).

Exploring teenage pregnancy and media representations of 'chavs'. Hetty Frampton explored the influence of class tensions in relation to news media representations of teenage pregnancy with particular reference to contemporary notions of the 'chav' figure. Her central discussion is based on an analysis of a small number of pertinent articles in two British newspapers (*The Daily Mail* and *The Guardian*) in conjunction with feminist theories of motherhood. She concludes that the construction of the 'chav' mum as a source of hilarity and disgust, and the subsequent everyday, instinctive responses towards class and teenage motherhood, need to be assessed further and recognized as direct constructions of image and identity (Frampton, 2010).

Perceived division of labor and work-family conflict among U.S. married and cohabiting women in heterosexual couples. Genevie Co aimed to determine whether married women differed from cohabiting women in levels of perceived fairness of the division of household and paid labour and also whether they differed in the amount of conflict between family life and paid work. Her study was a secondary analysis of data from a nationally representative US sample (the Married and Cohabiting Couples online survey). The sample used for this study consists of 691 women, with cases in the original study excluded if they were men or, among married participants, they cohabited prior to marriage. There were no statistically significant differences between married women and cohabiting women in the likelihood of either perceiving an unfair division of labour or reporting conflict between family life and paid work (Co & Nieri, 2012).

6. Internet-based Research Methods

Nature in the city: Young people's perceptions, values and experiences. Gillian Mayo sought to evaluate the knowledge which underpins official understandings of nature and to examine young people's attitudes and feelings towards the natural environment. Her primary data was gathered through an online questionnaire survey from a random sample of people aged 18–24 recruited from within the urban core, supplemented by other methods including a focus group discussion and semi-structured interviews. Secondary data was gathered through analysis of documents representing both governmental and non-governmental organizations and stakeholders (Mayo, 2010).

Twitter: a quantitative, semantic content analysis of the top 10 Twitter brands. Charlotte Vogelsinger analysed tweets from 10 top brands (Dunkin Donuts, Marvel, Starbucks, etc.) according to the type of tweet (Dialogue, ReTweet, Link, Picture, Video, etc.) and its content (Promotion, Customer Service, etc.) over two periods of time. She reviewed changes in the number of followers and trends in the type of tweets (Vogelsinger, 2010).

Physical intimacy and equity in the maintenance of college students' romantic relationships. Andrea Turtenwald in a qualitative study used snowball sampling to gather 10 heterosexual couples who had been exclusively dating for at least six months. Each partner was responsible for answering nine separate open-ended surveys online to describe their relationship in their own words and in relation to seven maintenance behaviours indicated by previous research. Numerous couples in the study emphasized equality in sacrifices and tasks in their relationship, supplementing the findings in previous research (Turtenwald, 2012).

Note: See also the section on 'Researching internet topics' in Chapter 3, p. 62.

Using More Than One Method

It is easiest to make one method central to a small-scale project. Perhaps it's essentially an interview-based project or mainly based on postal questionnaires, or whatever. Experiments typically have specialized methods specific to particular topics. Focusing your efforts on one method means that you can afford to spend the time needed to get on top of the practicalities of its use.

However, even in a small project, there is much to be said for devoting a small proportion of your time and effort to collecting some data by a different method. This will almost inevitably give you a somewhat different perspective on the data you get from the main method. In research jargon, this is called triangulation of methods, after the way in which a surveyor gets a 'fix' on position by approaching it from different angles.

One straightforward combination is to have documentary analysis as a secondary data collection method. In many situations, when doing research outside the laboratory, it helps to have 'sticky fingers' picking up copies of various documents in the setting where your project is based. Unless these are freely available documents (such as a prospectus, booklet or leaflet), you must get permission, of course.

It is also often possible to conduct some relatively informal interviews as a secondary method. Incorporating this type of data collection into a laboratory experiment, for example, can, with little cost of time and effort, give an invaluable participant's perspective on the experiment.

Mixed Method Designs

Something of a bandwagon has started rolling in recent years for what are usually called mixed method designs. Possibly linked to signs of the end of warfare between proponents of quantitative and qualitative research, this movement argues for research designs involving substantial elements of both types of approach in the same project. I prefer the term *multiple strategy* (Robson, 2011; Chapter 11) because the mixing of methods from the same stable (say interviewing and participant observation in a flexible design) is straightforward and not new. However, the very different mind-sets associated with fixed and flexible design research makes this type of project problematic for a lone researcher, rather than a team with a range of skills – particularly so for the novice student researcher.

Nevertheless, if you are interested in designs of this kind, it is well worth spending some time reading about their advantages. If your regulations allow it, one possibility is to work with a colleague where each of you has prime responsibility for one aspect of the design.

Data Collection Methods Used in Different Approaches

Box 2.5 shows the main data collection methods typically used with different approaches. Case study is unusual, as good practice is considered to call for two or more methods of data collection. In other traditions there has usually been a preferred main method of data collection.

Trustworthiness and Credibility

Whatever data collection method, or methods, that you use, you need to have a defence against a reader (or examiner) who asks, 'Why should I believe you?' when looking at your data and the way you have interpreted the findings.

I assume that, as stressed earlier in the chapter, p. 19, you are approaching this task seriously and honestly. Any cheats who make up or fiddle data, please leave now.

How do you seek to persuade the reader that what you are saying is worthy of trust? Your account is credible, or believable, largely through its general quality, including full details of what you did, and why you did it. There are, traditionally, two specific concerns associated with the data you collect. Are they reliable? Are they valid?

Reliability

The data collection method is reliable if you get essentially the same data when the measurement is repeated under the same conditions. If you start thinking about how this might be assessed, some logical and practical

Box 2.5 Data collection methods used in different approaches

	Likely main data collection method(s)	Possible secondary data collection method(s)
Action research	Interviews, participant observation.	Documentary analysis.
Case study	Multiple (often includes interviews, observation and documentary analysis).	
Ethnographic approach	Participant observation.	Documentary analysis, interviews.
Grounded theory approach	Interviews, participant observation.	Documentary analysis.
Experimental approach	Typically specially designed instrument (often structured observation, questionnaire or test).	Informal interviews.
Survey	Structured questionnaires or interviews, possibly structured observation.	Informal interviews.
Evaluation research	Any (depends on purpose of evaluation).	Documentary analysis.

problems come to the fore. It is virtually impossible to get an exact repetition of a measurement when you are working with people. Even when using a highly standardized method such as a questionnaire or some type of test, a question asked again to see if you get the same response, has logically to be at a different point in time. By then, the situation, or your respondent, may have changed in some way. The very fact that a question is repeated may lead to a different answer out of perversity or boredom.

When using standardized methods of data collection, it is usually feasible to get some reasonable reassurance about reliability. For example, using structured observation it is possible to have two observers. The test is whether or not they independently produce very similar results when observing the same situation. This is known as high inter-observer reliability. To get to this stage, it is often necessary to have lengthy periods of training of the observers. When questionnaires or scales are used, it is possible to have alternative versions of the questions or test items which you try to make sure are equivalent. Again, if the two versions produce essentially equivalent patterns of data from those responding, it demonstrates reliability.

Researchers who prefer flexible designs, and the use of methods which produce qualitative data, consider the whole idea of reliability somewhat dubious. They argue that they are dealing with complex and messy real-life situations, where highly standardized data collection methods are neither appropriate nor feasible. While accepting the force of this argument, it still leaves readers legitimately worried about whether they can rely on the data that have been collected. Tactics such as providing very full, 'thick' descriptions, which include the context in which observations are made, provide some reassurance. The use of triangulation (e.g. collecting data by different methods, from different informants, and from different types of informant), can also help.

Validity

Validity refers to whether or not something actually measures what it claims to measure. A measure can be reliable without being valid. For example, a test which purports to measure suitability for a particular job might be highly reliable in that the same people get the same scores when tested twice, but be useless at predicting later performance on the job. If it's not reliable, it can't be valid.

Validity is a worry whatever approach or method is used. There are technical, often complex, methods for assessing various types of validity when structured data collection methods are used (see Further Reading, p. 57).

Research Arguments

Above and beyond these technical issues, you answer the 'Why should I believe that?' question by the quality of the research argument presented in the report of your findings. This is the claim you make (typically in the form of answers to the research questions), linked to the evidence and reasons you present. This is discussed in detail in the final chapter.

In order to be in a position to present this argument in the report, you need to anticipate having to do this throughout the research process. It helps if you work at a draft of the report at an early stage. Much research is confirmatory. That is, you have a pretty good idea of what your findings are likely to be before the complete data are collected. This puts the onus on you to look actively for contrary evidence, i.e. findings which will contradict or disconfirm your expectations. Anticipating possible findings helps you to home in on the kinds of evidence which will strengthen your research argument. And to make sure that you look for this evidence while collecting data.

Even in a flexible exploratory study, where you don't have strong prior expectations, early data collection will begin to throw up ideas about the likely findings. It helps to shape the ways in which your data collection evolves. Again, your task is to try to collect data which will support the research argument you will eventually present.

Further Reading

Robson, C. (2011). Real world research: A resource for users of social research methods in applied settings (3rd ed.). Chichester, W. Sussex.: Wiley.

A 'big' text, useful if you feel that you need a more extensive background to different ways of doing research using social research methods.

Other relevant texts likely to be found in many academic libraries include the following. Earlier editions are worth consulting if the latest one is not available:

Bryman, A. (2012). *Social research methods* (4th ed.). Oxford, Oxon.: Oxford University Press.

Cohen, L., Manion, L., & Morrison, K. (2011). *Research methods in education* (7th ed.). Abingdon, Oxon.: Routledge.

Sarantakos, S. (2012) *Social research* (4th ed.). Basingstoke, Hants.: Palgrave Macmillan.

Chapter 2 Tasks

1 *Write into your project diary any ideas* which have come to you as a result of reading this chapter (the same applies to the following chapters, so I won't keep repeating it). In particular, note any revisions to your original thoughts about what you might do and first thoughts about how you might do it, arising from reading this chapter.

Don't push this though if you aren't at all sure. The next chapter concentrates on getting your ideas into focus.

2 *Prepare for action.* Before you get into the hurly-burly of doing the project, it is a good idea to get yourself sorted out on as many dimensions as possible. I like to think of a research project as a 'little life'. You are starting out with a clean slate (not really, but it helps to think that you are) and you have the opportunity of being well organized and prepared, on top of things, etc. For example:

☐ *Clear your deck/desk.* Sorting out your personal circumstances so that you have the physical and mental space to put your best efforts into the project.
☐ *Get your computer in good order.* Make sure you have the software you need, and know how to use it efficiently. In particular, set up arrangements to maintain back-ups of the word-processing and other files that arise from the project. Don't be one of those unfortunate people who have a hard disk crash when finishing the project report – and haven't got a copy of the final version somewhere safe.

3

Developing Your Ideas

Selecting a Topic

The selection of a general topic area tends either to be straightforward and quick, or problematic and likely to eat up a lot of valuable time – unless you are careful. It is easy if you are following up on something you have already been involved with, or if the topic is decided by someone else. If your supervisor says 'select one from this list', that's what you do – although, if you are really keen on doing something else, it is worth trying to persuade them.

In other situations, you need to give topic selection careful thought. Possibilities include things that interest you in lecture courses or seminars, or when you are getting material together for course assignments – go back to the notes you made. Talk to people – colleagues, fellow students, your supervisor. Read voraciously. Dip into recent issues of academic and professional journals, serious newspapers and magazines. Follow up tentative ideas on the internet using Google or a similar search engine (see the section on sources later in the chapter, p. 67).

A good early reality check is to look at recent examples of research project reports produced by recent graduates following the same course as yourself, if they are available. If they are not kept in your department or the library, finding some relevant research reports can be a part of your search for sources as covered on p. 67. Just try to get a general feel of what they look like and the kinds of topics that have been chosen. The examples taken from undergraduate research journals in Chapter 2, Boxes 2.2 (pp. 33–40) and 2.4 (pp. 46–53) give further ideas of what might be feasible.

Your topic should fulfil four main criteria:

1. *It interests you.* Doing a piece of research can be a very fulfilling experience. Many students consider it to be the most valuable and worthwhile part of their whole degree course. However, it can be frustrating. All sorts of

things can go wrong and some will. Having a real interest in the topic can keep you going through the inevitable sticky patches.

2. *It will meet course requirements.* As a student on a course, your primary audience is whoever will assess your work. There will be formal requirements about what is expected. These will mainly affect the type of study and how it is to be written up, rather than its focus.

3. *It will be feasible for you to deliver something worthwhile on the topic given the available time and resources.* Keep away from 'big' topics such as world peace or global warming. Though if something big really interests you, it may be feasible to focus on a particular small facet which is manageable.

4. *If it will require access to some particular setting is it likely to be granted?* This needs checking at a very early stage. Even if this appears possible, it can take a long time to get approval (see Chapter 4, p. 89).

There is a further criterion worth bearing in mind. Some topics and research questions are best addressed using a particular approach. You may have found some of the approaches and research traditions listed in Chapter 2 particularly interesting or attractive. Or have dismissed others as not for you. As pointed out in that chapter the important thing is to get a good match between topics, research questions and the type of project you feel comfortable with.

Beware highly sensitive topics. Lacking experience, you may be out of your depth and cause harm. For example, a study of an innovatory scheme for drug users, unless carefully handled, may stimulate opposition and cause its termination.

Advisers may also recommend that you keep away from currently 'hot' topics; i.e. ones where there is much current interest. However, if you can come up with something new and different which fulfils the criteria, and/or you have useful access, consider going for it. Even popular areas like these are rarely fully worked out. The main practical disadvantage is that you will need to get on top of a substantial amount of recently completed, perhaps not very accessible, research.

A fairly common situation is to come up with two possible 'runners' which you can't decide between. Then, when you find out more about the first topic, you begin to appreciate its problems, and so the second topic seems more attractive. And when you find out more about the second topic . . . And so on. Go for the one which interests you more.

Box 3.1 lists a varied set of topics mainly harvested from an hour's surfing on the internet. The last two are derived from Dunbar (2005), who provides a rich source of interesting topics, based on case studies in the evaluation of research designs.

Box 3.1 Examples of broad topic areas

Pets in sheltered housing for the elderly
Overcoming computer anxiety
Children and dinosaurs
Nanny care and language development
Homeless youth
Driving while talking on a mobile phone
Influence of TV lifestyle programmes
Educating children with behaviour problems in regular classes
Binge drinking
Graphology and job selection
Effects of video gaming

The internet provides an invaluable tool to explore a topic. While the usual warnings about the quality of material on the internet apply, they are not as important when you are just looking for ideas, so by all means get Googling – and using Google Scholar gives some reassurance as it is has a focus on 'academic' material – journal articles, conference reports, reports, books, etc.

For example, "Overcoming computer anxiety", using double quotation marks to search for that exact phrase, gave me 49 results (hits) with Google Scholar, "Children and dinosaurs" 12 hits. Searching for some topics you may draw a blank. There were no results for "Pets in sheltered housing for the elderly" with Google Scholar or with the standard Google. A tactic here is to make the topic less specific. You could try removing the double quotation marks. This gave 244 results from Scholar for articles with combinations of 'pets', 'sheltered housing' and 'elderly' somewhere in the text.

With "Homeless youth" you have the reverse problem as Google Scholar produced 11,000 results. Here the problem is to see the wood for the trees, but there are usually fairly obvious pointers toward possible facets of the topic which might be more manageable. Reviewing some of the results should help. Perhaps "preschool homeless children" (19 results), or 'compensatory education programs for homeless school-age children' (removing the double quotation marks) which gave 130 results.

What you are after in these searches are ideas about the kinds of things you might focus on if you decide to select this topic. You don't need many leads. Many topics can yield a worthwhile and feasible project with sufficient ingenuity and focusing.

Researching internet topics

The internet and associated digital phenomena such as iPhones, Facebook, YouTube and other social media form such an important part of many people's lives that they are obvious candidates for the focus of a research project. Examples of topics selected by undergraduates for their project include:

- ☐ the online experiences of adolescents – McGivern & Noret (2011)
- ☐ the use of podcasts for learning English – Li (2010)
- ☐ online shopping behaviour – Kramer (2012), and
- ☐ the role of the internet in donor insemination – Wheatley (2010).

Research topics to avoid

There are topics you should steer clear of. For example, topics which are:

- ☐ *Too big.* Topics which demand more resources to complete in the time that you have available. Can be rescued by focusing on one aspect only.
- ☐ *Too trivial.* New researchers, frightened by warnings about limited resources, can go to the opposite extreme. Small can be beautiful; some high-quality projects research a single unit such as a classroom. But there has to be compensating depth and detail. Avoid the trivial. A very specific topic should be defensible as having some kind of wider relevance, to practice, theory, or whatever.
- ☐ *Too difficult.* Just because you can isolate an interesting topic, doesn't mean you can say anything worthwhile about it. There may be good reasons why a topic hasn't been previously researched.
- ☐ *Too boring.* Avoid a topic that doesn't interest you. Even if you complete it (and you might find it difficult to maintain motivation), others are also likely to find it boring.
- ☐ *Ethically dubious.* Steer clear of topics which you can't do without breaching ethical guidelines (e.g. putting participants at risk of harm, or where findings might be used to harm or disadvantage someone). See p. 76.

🕸 *The website (www.wiley.com/college/robson) gives links to material on topic selection*

Replication research

A replication of a piece of research is an attempt to repeat it. In social research there is much concern about the replicability of findings from previous research; i.e. whether repeating the research would result in the same findings. A distinction is made between exact replications, which, as the term suggests, seek to repeat the study exactly, and constructive replications in which the original study is modified in one or more respects.

If you are interested in the findings of a piece of research you have come across, or if the findings seem suspect, there is much to be said for attempting a constructive replication of it. Not an exact replication, as it might be argued that there is not enough of you in the exercise. Also your study probably couldn't be an exact replication anyway, as it necessarily takes place at a different time from the original, and probably in a context which differs in other important aspects. Check that a study of this type is acceptable in your course regulations.

From a Topic to Research Questions

Your first task is to move from the broad topic area to a more focused topic. Think of this as your working title for the project. It is often helpful to have a two-part title, e.g. 'Why do children like dinosaurs? An exploratory study at a nursery school'. Or 'I couldn't take my cat: A study of policies in residential homes for the elderly, and their effects'. One part indicates the topic area. The other tells you something about the focus.

The second, crucial, and difficult, task is to formulate the research questions to which your project will try to get answers. Resist the temptation to go out and collect data until you have at least a tentative set of possible questions.

In coming to a decision to go for a topic, and from the reading and discussions you have had along the way, you will probably already have an initial set of questions that you can write down. They are likely to be of different types. Some may be nuts-and-bolts questions of the 'who/what/where/when' kind (some 'why' ones wouldn't go amiss, either). Make a list of any and all questions you can come up with. Splurge – don't censor them for whether or not they are sensible. Box 3.2 gives an example.

This set of 20 questions is typical of most 'splurged' lists in being something of a mess. There are many more questions than one could hope to deal with adequately in a small-scale project; it is very teacher-oriented, and there is considerable overlap between several of the questions. Nevertheless, it is a useful starting point.

From Research Questions to a Research Design

The general topic of the use of interactive whiteboards (i.e. large screens on which the teacher can not only produce and show written material, but also

Box 3.2 An initial (unedited) set of research questions

1 How do teachers in secondary schools use interactive 'whiteboards'?
2 What training have teachers had in the use of interactive 'whiteboards'?
3 Which teaching subjects are interactive 'whiteboards' most useful for?
4 Which pupil ages are interactive 'whiteboards' most useful for?
5 Which ability groups are interactive 'whiteboards' most useful for?
6 Does the use of interactive 'whiteboards' by teachers vary with the age and experience of the teacher?
7 What do teachers consider to be the advantages of interactive 'whiteboards'?
8 What do teachers consider to be the disadvantages of interactive 'whiteboards'?
9 What factors affect the extent to which teachers use interactive 'whiteboards'?
10 What are the difficulties in using interactive 'whiteboards'?
11 Why are some teachers reluctant to use interactive 'whiteboards' in their classroom?
12 Which teachers make very intensive use of interactive 'whiteboards'?
13 Has the availability of interactive 'whiteboards' changed the teaching style of teachers?
14 Are there factors currently inhibiting the use of interactive 'whiteboards' in the classroom?
15 Which teachers have access to interactive 'whiteboards'?
16 On what basis are teachers chosen to have access to interactive 'whiteboards'?
17 Does the head teacher's attitude to interactive 'whiteboards' influence their implementation in a school?
18 What changes in use of the interactive 'whiteboards' have occurred since their introduction?
19 What views do pupils have about interactive 'whiteboards'?
20 Would the money spent on interactive 'whiteboards' be better spent on other things?

where pictures, DVDs, websites and interactive material can be displayed) in the school classroom, could be approached using many different research designs. The questions provide pointers to the design, the type and style of the project and which method(s) of data collection might be appropriate.

Several of the questions, for example, questions 2 to 5 inclusive, and 7 to 10 inclusive, suggest some kind of teacher survey. Question 11 might best be addressed by interviewing teachers. Question 1, and probably questions 12 and 14 to 17 inclusive, and question 19 suggest some observational study in schools, coupled with interviews with pupils, teachers and the head teacher. Questions 13 and 18 would ideally call for some type of longitudinal study with researcher involvement in the school(s) for a period before the introduction of whiteboards and over the next year or so after their introduction.

Thinking about your splurged set of research questions helps you to take a step back and consider not only the broad overall topic, but also what the purpose of your project is going to be. Perhaps you now appreciate that, at this stage at least, you just don't know enough about the situation in schools to do anything other than an exploratory study. This will effectively rule out a fixed design project and push toward a flexible design.

However, if you have recent school experience, or find relevant research studies, then a fixed design project such as a survey or some kind of field experiment or quasi-experiment might well be feasible. Once decisions like this have been made, you can start pruning and generally tailoring your research question list so that it fits in with the focus you have, provisionally, decided on.

You still have more research question work to do. The main task is to decide which are the main research questions. This doesn't stop you retaining some additional subsidiary questions, though you may well find that you have to drop some questions from the list at a later stage because you won't have the time and resources to get answers to them.

One research question or several?

Some project reports only mention a single research question. I find this too restricting and that there are always several which crop up when you are thinking about a possible project. Certainly there is nothing wrong with having a single main question and other less central ones.

Do I really need research questions?

Not if you don't find them useful. Some researchers find this an unnecessarily constricting way of working. They prefer to decide on a focus of their research, go out and collect data, then see what they can make of what they have. Provided you follow the 'systematically/sceptically/ethically' rubric outlined at the start of Chapter 2, p. 20, I wouldn't wish to warn you off following this tack. Certainly, you will find many published accounts of research which are not presented in terms of research questions (although this doesn't necessarily mean that they didn't use research questions when actually doing the study).

I hold firmly to the belief that sorting out a coherent set of research questions, while it can be difficult, pays dividends. Provided you don't regard them as set in stone, where you have to stick with an initial set of questions, they can be adapted to virtually all styles of research from rigidly pre-specified designs to very flexible ones.

Part II of this book is concerned with the data collection part of the project. For this you need to be armed with your initial set of research questions. I have suggested that your interest in a topic should be the main driver in its selection and in working out related research questions. However, in practice, it can often be more complicated. In particular, after reading Chapter 2 on general approaches and data collection methods and your previous knowledge and experience, your feelings about them legitimately come into play. As do practicalities of time and resources, including access opportunities and difficulties.

As stressed on p. 23, it is crucial that the general approach and data collection methods you choose are appropriate for finding answers to your research questions, and that you have the resources and access necessary. If not, something must change – possibly the topic and/or one or more research questions.

Don't forget that the task is not just to get some research questions, but also to seek answers to them. It is not unknown for a report to list the questions, but not get round to providing an explicit discussion of the answers obtained as a result of doing the research.

Hypotheses

In some areas of research, there are strong traditions of talking in terms of hypotheses. In a general sense, 'having a hypothesis' about something means having a provisional, or tentative, explanation of what is going on. Thinking in this way can do nothing but good. It gives direction to your research and helps to suggest research questions.

There is a more restricted use of the term within the so-called hypothetico–deductive approach. Here the notion is that you start with a theory from which one or more hypotheses are derived. And the central purpose of the research is to test the hypotheses. There can be a whole apparatus of null hypotheses and alternative hypotheses, often linked to an elaborate statistical technology for deciding between them. As I have already indicated, my own preference is to regard the research task as one of getting answers to questions rather than testing hypotheses. It has the advantage of applying to virtually all approaches to research, without strait-jacketing you into one particular view of the nature of research.

It may be that you are researching in an area, or following an approach, where this hypothesis approach rules supreme. Your preparatory reading, particularly of journals, will reveal this – and your supervisor will no doubt make this clear. If so, you had better go with the flow. Many standard texts give the rules (e.g. Coolican, 2014).

Developing the Design

Let's assume that, as a result of your preliminary reading and discussion with others (not least your supervisor), you have a pretty clear idea of the topic and focus of your project, of the approach you want to take and that you have initial thoughts about research questions.

At this stage, the priority is to find out as much as you can about what others have already established, through research and review, relevant to your proposed project. This task forms the basis for the next section on finding and using sources. Be warned. It is not unknown for students to get so absorbed in searching for sources that they leave themselves insufficient time for actually carrying out the research, let alone writing it up. You also need to give serious attention at this early stage to the possible ethical implications of the proposed project. This is covered in the section Ethical considerations (p. 74).

Finding and Using Sources

'Sources' are materials, and people, that can help you with your research project. The main concern here is to use such sources to give you ideas about how you should design your study. Has someone done a study which you can use as a model? Are there problems you haven't thought of? Or do you come across a study which leads to your thinking about the whole topic differently?

This isn't the only function of sources when doing a research project. For example, you will need them to provide backing for the claims you make when interpreting your data. Sources should inform every phase of the project and every aspect of your final report.

You are not alone when doing research, even though it may sometimes feel like that. The shadow army of all those who have done research and written about it are at your disposal. The trick is in finding relevant material. Your supervisor should help to get you going. Supervisors are themselves, of course, potentially very useful sources in their own right. This is particularly so if you are following a topic that they have suggested and which links into their research interests.

The 'literature review' is often a required part of a research report. It provides an account of previous research which has been carried out, together with attempts which have been made to provide frameworks within which the research can be placed and understood. All too often, such reviews degenerate into an ill-digested listing of an inordinate number of references, which simply demonstrates that many more or less relevant sources have been unearthed by the writer. The section on 'research arguments' in Chapter 6, p. 134 makes suggestions about how you can structure the review.

Less can be more. In other words, there is greater value in homing in on a relatively small number of really key references, and giving a full account of what they contribute and why it is relevant to your own study. However, if the powers that be insist on a review stuffed with many references, give them what they want. You should still ensure that you have sufficient space to do justice to what you consider to be the key references.

You will already have done some reading around when deciding on the topic of your research. If you are lucky, there might be one reference, perhaps a section in a book, or a review article on a particular field, or a journal account of a piece of research, which seems spot on.

Planning the search for sources

How do you start? Your efforts in deciding on a focus for the research will have thrown up an initial set of sources, whether suggested by your supervisor, or from books, research reviews, journal articles, newspapers or other media, or whatever. To take this further, there are two main avenues; the internet and libraries. You can get away with just using one of these if you have to. However, although the internet is an amazingly rich resource, don't neglect the library and its librarians. An academic library is a wonderful resource – you should know by this stage of your course how to make full use of its resources. If not, it isn't too late. And serendipity, that happy knack of making fortunate discoveries, is a wonderful thing – the next book along on the shelf, or another paper in the journal rather than the one you were seeking, can prove to be a key source.

Key word searching

Develop a set of key words to help you organize the search. Most journal articles include them. For example, in a journal report based on her undergraduate project, Mairena Hirschberg studied living with chronic illness (Hirschberg, 2012) and used the keywords 'chronic illness, social participation, sociology of health and medicine, public sphere, private sphere, quantitative methods, and General Household Survey'. In her project, Marjolein Kramer studying online shopping behaviour (Kramer, 2012) used 'e-shopping, apparel, theory of reasoned action, structural equation modelling, attitude, internet search, and subjective norm', while Ruari Sutherland in a comparison of the activities and development of the English and Scottish Defence Leagues (Sutherland, 2012) had as keywords 'English Defence League, Scottish Defence League, nationalism, and racism'.

Using key words which seem obvious from the title of your project, together with ones that you glean from some relevant articles, should get you an initial set which you refine and modify as you go about your search. Many of the resources available via library catalogues or the internet make use of key word searching and you should make sure you can do this efficiently (there's usually a 'help' button which gives the rules).

A very basic rule which usually applies is that if you get too few 'hits' when using individual search terms, then try one key word 'OR' a second key word; if too many, then a key word 'AND' a second one. If you find that a search returns many items of a particular type that you don't want, then use 'NOT' to exclude them.

When you do come across relevant sources, do make sure that you get a full reference for them. Make sure that you use the style required by your course regulations. A common style, used in many social science disciplines and applied areas, as well as psychology (and this book) is known as APA 6th (American Psychological Association, 2013).[*]

> The website (*www.wiley.com/college/robson*) gives links to material on reference styles used in different disciplines and referencing of electronic sources

Partial references (e.g. where you have left out authors' initials or page numbers for a journal reference) are a pain when you are writing up. Just a few of them can cause you hours of work finding the missing details.

Internet searching

The business of getting hold of sources has been revolutionized in the last few years by the development of the internet. You can search for sources by traditional means using resources physically present in academic libraries.

---

[*] This differs considerably from the 5th edition. There are minor differences in the various guides to it. The main thing is to ensure that your use of a reference style is consistent throughout.

This kind of search still has a place, as discussed in the following section. However, it is perverse not to take advantage of the vast range of material now easily accessible via the internet.

Beware! As you should already be well aware there is a major problem in sorting out the valuable information from the huge amount of questionable quality dross. Take advantage of any sessions available in your library to develop skills in dealing with this problem. There is excellent material on the web itself in the form of the 'Virtual Training Suite' – a set of free internet tutorials to help university students develop internet research skills written and reviewed by a national team of lecturers and librarians from universities across the UK (http://www.vtstutorials.co.uk/).

The 'academic' Google Scholar (www.scholar.google.com) can often turn up items not available in other searches, including unpublished reports, conference proceedings and theses. These can contain the kind of detail on procedures not found in journal articles, which is particularly useful when designing a project. However, they still need to be carefully evaluated from a quality point of view, and are sometimes early drafts which have subsequently been modified on publication (search to see whether a published version exists).

The use of Wikipedia is controversial in academic circles, with some university departments banning the use of references from it in project reports and other assessed work. It has contributions from many (unnamed) authors and it is difficult to assess how authoritative the information is.[†] Even if your department does not have an explicit ban, it is safer to avoid relying directly on anything from Wikipedia in your project report – and not to use it as a reference. Quoting from Wikipedia while not referencing it is, of course, plagiarism.

Library searching

One great thing that libraries have in their favour is librarians. They can lead you to the range of resources (including internet resources) available in and through the libraries. Subject librarians in academic libraries are often mines of information which will help you in your searches. Take advantage of any training courses going. Resources such as databases (e.g. BIDS, Web of Science, ERIC) including citation indices (e.g. SSCI – the Social Science Citation Index) are now typically available in disk-based and web-based

---

[†] Rishi Chandy (an undergraduate student) provides an interesting account of the tools and tactics used to identify and counteract propaganda in Wikipedia entries (Chandy, 2008).

versions. Citation indices are useful. A reference you think is key to your project may well have been cited by others following its publication. A citation index lets you check this.

Books and print journals remain an important library resource. Keyword searches through the library catalogue will help you to find where relevant books are located. Inter-library loans will get you texts not in your own library, but can take a considerable time to come through. There is a multitude of journal article subject bibliographies through which you can search. There will probably be a small number of journals where many of the articles from your searches are found. Have a good browse through the last few years' issues and particularly the 'current parts' which can be in a different section of a library. Revisit them when you are writing up as you may well find that something new has just been published which you should know about.

Dealing with the sources

Once you have found some sources (books, journal articles or whatever) which look promising, the next task is to sort them out in some way.

One approach is to order them into three piles (either real or virtual piles depending on whether you are dealing with paper or electronic sources) – 'key'; 'useful'; and 'useless':

1. *Key sources* are ones which are central to your topic and research questions. Perhaps ones which you can use as a model for your own efforts, or which suggest a next step. In my experience, you will be lucky to come up with more than half a dozen of these.
2. *Useful sources* are ones which you may want to take note of in some way. Perhaps in the design of your project, or simply by referring to them in your report.
3. *Useless sources* are ones which on first glance looked relevant but further reading reveals that they aren't. Don't throw them away; your project might change and develop in ways that make them relevant. Keep them separately so that they don't clutter up your active set of sources.

Sorting a long list of 'possibles' can take a long time. Good reading skills help. If you are a slow reader, consider spending some time to increase your speed. Useful reading techniques include:

☐ *Skimming* A rapid dash through the source to try to get an impression of whether there are any ideas or information you might use and to decide if it is relevant.

☐ *Scanning.* Another rapid dash but this time looking for a specific item. Does it have anything about X? You ignore everything else. However I often find that something I wasn't looking for attracts my attention – and turns out to be valuable.

Reading for understanding. Once you have made the decision that a source is likely to be useful, possibly a key source, then you need to study it in some detail to ensure that you understand it. This study might be limited to a short passage, or a chapter in a book, or the whole of a journal article or book. For anything longer than a short passage, it helps to focus initially on its main features. For a book this could be:

☐ reading the preface
☐ checking the contents table, and
☐ reading any introductions to chapters and chapter summaries (if there aren't any, skim through each chapter, noting the major sections it is divided into).

For a journal article:

☐ reading the abstract
☐ reading the introductory and concluding sections, and
☐ noting the major sections.

Now you have a feeling for the lie of the land, the hard work starts. While the source may not have actually set explicit research questions, an approach I find helpful is to ask: What are the questions (or problems) they are trying to address? And what are the answers (or solutions) they have come up with? Some sources focus on a single main question, but there will typically be several subsidiary questions lurking around.

Note making. You need to have a record of each source that you are likely to make use of. At a minimum, this involves the information to be included in the bibliography or reference list at the end of your report (see Chapter 6, p. 139). Make sure that you record and store this information for each source that you are likely to use, immediately that you decide it may be useful. As already stressed, it can be a major pain, and cost much time and effort, chasing up missing references when completing your report.

There is specialized bibliographic software, likely to be available via your library, which can be very helpful if you have to deal with a lot of references. Zotero (http://www.zotero.org), a free, very easy to use tool which can electronically capture the reference details (and often the abstracts as well) of journal articles in e-journals, can save much fiddly typing.

Making additional notes about a source is very much a personal decision. Some people feel that they never understand something unless and until they have expressed it in their own words. Others spend many happy hours highlighting or underlining large chunks of their copy. This is mainly an issue with your small set of key references. You do need to know them well and undoubtedly you demonstrate this understanding to yourself and others by writing your own account. And this understanding may be central to the way you design and carry out your project. However, it is in your report of the project that you have to incorporate discussion of the various sources and their relevance to your project and you may be making better use of your precious time by writing drafts of parts of the report.

🕸 *The website (www.wiley.com/college/robson) gives links to material on finding and using sources*

Getting an Overall Picture

By now you should have accumulated a good number of individual pieces of information from your reading. This is a good time to think about the overall picture. You need to get some kind of record about your ideas and how they might fit together. Useful techniques include 'spider diagrams' and what is usually called a 'concept map' or 'mind map'. The latter is usually made up of labelled boxes with links between them. Box 3.3 shows how to do this.

Box 3.3 Constructing a concept map

1 Brainstorm the concepts

  ☐ From your notes list any and all terms and concepts associated with your project topic.
  ☐ Write them on Post-It notes, one word or phrase per note.
  ☐ Don't worry about redundancy, importance, or relationships between them.

2 Organize the concepts

  ☐ Spread the notes out on a table.
  ☐ Create groups and sub-groups of related items. Try to group items to emphasize hierarchies. Identify terms that represent higher categories and add them.

☐ Rearrange the notes, deleting and introducing new items until you are happy with the result.

3 Draw the map with each concept in a separate box

☐ Use a consistent hierarchy with the most important concepts in the centre or at the top.
☐ Within sub-groupings, place closely related items near each other.
☐ Use lines with arrows to connect and show the relationship between connected items. Many arrows can originate or terminate on particularly important concepts.
☐ Write a word or short phrase beside each arrow to specify the relationship.

Some people include their concept map in the project report – probably modified from this first attempt in the light of how the project actually turned out. If you are doing this make sure that its presentation is to a professional standard. Concept maps are not difficult to produce using PowerPoint or specialist software (e.g. a free version associated with Google Chrome, who also provide SpiderNote).

🕸 *The website (www.wiley.com/college/robson) gives links to material with examples of concept maps*

Ethical Considerations

Carrying out any form of research can have an effect on people in a wide variety of ways. Indeed, it might be argued that there is little point to research involving people if it doesn't have the potential to affect someone in some way. Researchers are more likely to see the potential for good in their efforts, whether through increased understanding, more effective or efficient products, or some other positive contribution. However, even with entirely benign intentions, actual consequences can be negative, and possibly harmful, for those taking part in the research, or for those whose lives are affected by the results of the research. Unleashing the power of nuclear energy, or developing genetically modified crops, are commonly cited examples where researchers face difficult dilemmas.

Certainly, any research which involves people as participants in a project will be highly likely to raise ethical issues. Have their rights, autonomy, and sensitivities been respected? Is it possible that they will come to harm in some way as a result of their involvement? Do they know what they are letting themselves in for – in the jargon, have they given 'informed consent' (see Chapter 4, p. 86)?

Others, as well as the direct participants, could be affected by your research. Suppose your findings are used to justify the closure of a service or facility. Clients may suffer as a result. Or perhaps the findings are seen as justifying a new approach. Which may be fine if you have shown its benefits, but less so if its attraction is primarily because it is cheap.

Possible ethical issues arising from your project should be discussed with your supervisor at an early stage. For example, what do you do if a participant becomes distressed in an interview? While sensitive topics where distress is likely are best avoided by novice researchers, apparently innocuous topics can turn out to be upsetting for some participants. You need to be prepared. Perhaps stop the interview, turn off the recorder if you are using one and offer to talk it through if they would like to. Or offer a post-interview follow up.

Carrying out projects in outside organizations always raises issues. A proposal should be checked out for ethical issues as part of seeking approval to carry out the research from people within the organization. If they are keen on the project, particularly if they have suggested the topic, you need to satisfy yourself that they wish it to be carried out for ethically reputable reasons, and are not using you to legitimate something disreputable.

Formal ethical approval

It is good practice for there to be an 'ethics approval document' which has to be agreed with your supervisor, either making out the case for there being no ethical issues raised by the study, or giving details of the issues that are raised. In the UK it is likely to include a section on how you plan to meet the requirements of the Data Protection Act. Any ethical issues must then be thought through and the decision to proceed only made after it can be demonstrated that every effort has been made to reduce any likely harmful effects to a minimal level. And that these negative effects are likely to be outweighed by the potential benefits of the study.

Who makes this decision? Certainly not you. Nor should this be a decision made by researchers on their research proposals, even when they are vastly more experienced than you are.

Ethical committees

It is increasingly common for there to be a formal committee set up with responsibility for ethical approval, possibly combining this with more general powers of approval for the research proposal. Your supervisor should know the set-up and give advice about what is needed. Some types of proposal will need the go-ahead of more than one ethics committee (e.g. if you are working for an award at an academic institution and carrying out the research in a hospital or other health-related setting). This can be a pain if different committees have different requirements. Your supervisor should seek to sort this out and to establish where the proposal goes first.

Avoiding the unethical

Things which might be considered dubious on ethical grounds include:

- [ ] involving people without their knowledge, or without their explicit and informed consent
- [ ] exerting pressure to become involved in the research
- [ ] using deception about the purpose of the research, or what taking part involves
- [ ] exposing participants to ridicule or embarrassment, or otherwise injuring their self-esteem
- [ ] putting participants under physical or mental stress
- [ ] invading privacy or not respecting participants' autonomy, e.g. when seeking to change behaviour, attitudes, etc.
- [ ] giving benefits or rewards to some but not others, and
- [ ] treating people unfairly, or with lack of consideration or respect.

It is, however, difficult to sustain the argument that each of these practices should always be avoided. There are public situations where it is not feasible to ask for consent, nor to ensure that people even know that they are being focused on in a study (for example, in studies of car driver behaviour at traffic lights, or in the vicinity of speed cameras). Is the pressure exerted on students in some psychology degree courses to act as participants in departmental research projects unethical? Or is it legitimated as a social commitment appropriate for members of that department?

In some fields, notably social psychology, deception as to the purposes of the research was common. The argument put forward was that knowing the real purpose would preclude study of the phenomenon researched. Outright deception is rarely proposed in current research. A softer and more acceptable line involving 'honest but vague on details' is now more commonly taken. More generally, there is a welcome change of climate where what might be termed 'participants' rights' are taken more seriously. This is particularly so in research involving vulnerable groups such as children and persons with disabilities. However, horror stories still occur and there is continuing need for vigilance.

Explicitly asking participants if they are willing to take part in a project, knowing what this involves, and getting their approval – the principle of 'voluntary informed consent' – is now standard practice for research involving people (see Chapter 4, p. 86).

Moving beyond box-ticking

Ethical approval is sometimes treated as a box-ticking exercise with the project report simply certifying that the appropriate guidelines have been followed and ethical approval obtained. However, it is important to go beyond this and specify what was actually done in order to deal with ethical issues.

Jonathan Kelly, in a journal report of his undergraduate project on the ambitions of secondary school girls in Jinja District, Uganda provides an example (Kelly, 2011). He sought to make his involvement beneficial to the participants as well as himself by donating educational equipment to the schools involved. He was concerned about the effects of power imbalance and tried to mitigate this by adopting an informal interviewing style and giving the participants the choice of interview location. Kelly was careful to avoid causing them distress, for example, by not asking potentially emotive family questions and only enquiring about family issues if they were mentioned first by a participant. His interest in the lives of participants was matched by their interest in the life of the researcher and in 'what life is like in England'. Answering the questions of participants also helped to mitigate power imbalances and meant that they were able to gain something on a personal level from the interaction.

The website (www.wiley.com/college/robson) gives links to material on ethics and research ethics codes

Confirming Your Choices

Reading the material from the sources you have obtained, together with more thinking and discussion, should help you to firm up the likely detailed focus of your project. Does it look as if you will have to do an exploratory study because little relevant research appears to be available? Nothing wrong with doing a study in a new area, but is it something that you would feel comfortable with? If not, you will need to rethink, and refocus into an area where there is previous work that you can build on.

Has the reading confirmed what you thought were your research questions, or do you now consider something rather different would be more appropriate? As discussed earlier in the chapter (p. 63), the form of these questions provides pointers to the design.

Further Reading

Blaikie, N. (2009). *Designing social research: The logic of anticipation* (2nd ed.). Cambridge, Cambs.: Polity Press.

    Emphasis on the formulation of research questions and selection of an appropriate approach to answer them.

Hammersley, M., & Traianou, A. (2012). Ethics in qualitative research: Controversies and contexts. London: Sage.

    Timely text on a complex area. Focus on minimizing harm, respecting autonomy, and protecting privacy.

Sieber, J.E., & Tolich, M.B. (2013). *Planning ethically responsible research* (2nd ed.). Thousand Oaks, CA.: Sage.

    Focus on student projects and internal review boards.

Smith, M., & Williamson, E. (Eds.). (2004). *Researchers and their subjects: Ethics, power, knowledge and consent*. Bristol: The Policy Press.

    Case studies of proposals where ethical issues were central. Covers a wide range of disciplines.

White, P. (2009). *Developing research questions: A guide for social scientists*. Basingstoke, Hants.: Palgrave Macmillan.

    Short text focusing on turning ideas into researchable questions. Strongly recommended.

Chapter 3 Tasks

Following discussions with your supervisor, with colleagues (in the group if you've managed to set one up) and your reading:

1 *Firm up your choice of topic for the project.* You can still change it if, after further reading and thought, you don't think it will work out. But beware of wasting time over this.

2 *Get down a 'long list' of possible research questions.* Think of as many as you can in, say, half an hour. Invite suggestions and comments.

3 *Consider what kind of approach (case study, survey, etc.) might be appropriate for the different questions.* You should be able to group together questions which would call for the same approach.

4 *Decide, provisionally, on the main research questions.* Choose something which can be tackled by an approach you feel comfortable with, which will be feasible within your time and resource constraints, and which you find interesting.

5 *Find out as much as you can relevant to the topic and the research question(s).* Chase up relevant sources via the library and internet. The purpose of this search is to get ideas for the design of the project and to assess whether the provisional decisions you have made about focus and research questions need modifying. Set a time limit of a few days for this search (there's a danger that this gets so involving that you don't want to stop – don't forget that you actually have to carry out the project and write it up as well).

6 *Revisit your earlier decisions in the light of the search, and come up with a working title and the set of research questions with which you will start data collection.* These can still change right up to completing your report, depending on how things develop.

7 *Review ethical issues.* Write down the possible issues (using a document or form developed by your institution, if available) and discuss with your supervisor. Take advice about the need for formal ethical approval procedures.

and

8 *Consider whether it will be necessary to obtain access to do the research.* Take advice from your supervisor on this and on how access is to be requested. As obtaining agreement for access can be a lengthy process, start the process as soon as possible (see Chapter 4, p. 86).

Part II

Doing It

Sooner or later you are going to have to get down to collecting some data. Making the transition from preparation mode to action mode can be difficult for some. They persuade themselves that they're not quite ready, and need to do more reading. Or that they should think it over some more before committing themselves. Others are itching to get on with the real work and skimp on the preparation.

As discussed in Chapter 2, p. 23, fixed and flexible designs differ considerably in the degree of preparedness needed before you start on the main data collection exercise. With a fixed design, such as in survey or experimental research, meticulous pre-planning is essential. Part of this pre-planning is piloting, so that you can have confidence that what you are proposing is likely to be feasible. In flexible design studies it is neither possible nor desirable to get things tied down in advance to the same extent. You still need to have a broad focus or area of interest and some idea of where you are going both literally, (knowing the situation or site you will be involved with), and conceptually (having an initial, probably tentative and fluid, set of research questions). However, a central feature of flexible design research is that you allow things to evolve. How you proceed depends to a considerable extent on how things go. You follow up promising leads. Abandon blind alleys. Develop and refine your research questions as you appreciate more what is going on, and how it might be understood.

Practicalities of Data Collection

Once you have chosen the method(s) appropriate to the project, this, together with the decisions already made about research questions and the general style or approach you are going to adopt, puts in place the main building blocks of the project design. There are, of course, many detailed decisions to be made in preparing for and running the project. These include the 'who', 'what', 'where', and 'when' questions ('why' has already been addressed when considering the purpose of the project – to explore, explain or whatever, see Chapter 2, p. 20):

- [ ] *Who?* Which participants, and how many, are you going to select?
- [ ] *What and whe*re? Which settings should you choose for data collection? What kinds of setting and where geographically (and, again, how many)?
- [ ] *When?* What date do you start, and how long do you go on for?

Many of these questions may have pretty self-evident answers. The place where you collect data may be determined by the nature of the project. There may only be, say, a couple of weeks when the data have to be collected. There will usually be some freedom in who, and how many, you ask to participate. This is a sampling issue and is discussed in the following section.

In fixed designs, you run pilot studies which will, amongst other things, help you assess whether your plan is realistic. In flexible designs, you have to keep a continuing watching brief while collecting data. Can you afford to spend more time on promising aspects? Can you curtail aspects when time is short? Practicalities of this kind are discussed in the following sections.

Sampling and Sample Sizes

The 'who', 'what', 'where' and 'when' questions are essentially about sampling. You can't do everything so you have to be selective. In particular, limits have to be set on the number of participants you get involved with. In other words, you must select a sample of participants.

Some types of social research, notably the survey, rely heavily on this sample being representative of some wider population. If you have a representative sample it is then possible to make statistical generalizations about aspects of the population from what you find out in your study about the sample. These are always estimates, but it is possible to assess the likely degree of error in such estimates. Sample surveys are widespread, not only in research but in political polling and marketing. Their design and analysis can be sophisticated. In applied fields, there can be commercial implications of getting inaccurate results which helps ensure that the researchers get it right.

Representative samples

Suppose that you are carrying out a survey of student satisfaction in your college. The relevant population might be all those enrolled on courses on a particular date. A representative sample, where one can legitimately make generalizations from what one finds in the sample of students participating in your survey to the population of students in the college as a whole, would have to ensure that all enrolled students would have the same chance of being included in the sample. This is not an easy task.

The most straightforward way, conceptually, is to go for a simple random sample. To do this, you need a list of all students enrolled on the date that you have chosen (this list is called the sampling frame). Say that you decide on a 10 per cent sample. The traditional way of selecting the sample was to use some type of lottery approach (e.g. slips of paper each with a number representing a student on the list), or random number tables, where selections are made until you have your sample. 'Research Randomizer' (www.randomizer.org/) is a website which provides a very easy-to-use way of performing random sampling and is highly recommended. Follow their tutorial if in doubt.

Armed with your sample list of names (from their number codes), you proceed to contact them by post, e-mail, or whatever means you have decided. At this stage, you will encounter problems in getting hold of some of them – perhaps they have left, or there is a mistake in the list or whatever. It is advisable to select any necessary replacements in the same way that the original sample was selected. See the suggested Further Reading for the tactics to deal with these, and other, complexities.

A simple random sample of all students may not be the best way of approaching the selection of a sample. Perhaps your main interest is in students following a first degree course. If so you can simplify your task by making students on such courses your population. Suppose that you want to ensure that your sample includes reasonable numbers from each of the schools or departments in the university. Or from all courses. Or to make sure that the sample has the same proportion of male and female students as there are overall. It is feasible to cover issues like this by more complex sampling procedures, including cluster and stratified sampling (see Further Reading).

Non-probability samples

Small-scale research projects often do not attempt to use the ways of obtaining representative samples discussed above. Convenience samples are common where researchers grab hold of whoever they can; friends, relatives, fellow-students, passers-by, etc. There is nothing necessarily wrong or inappropriate in doing this, provided you make clear in your report what has been done. And provided that you do not claim that your findings are statistically generalizable in the way that random samples are. Experimental designs often use convenience samples. They rely on random assignment of participants to the different experimental conditions, which enables valid comparisons to be made between the conditions but still leaves their generalizability problematic.

Flexible design research projects commonly make use of purposive samples. Here, there is a deliberate attempt to select participants with known characteristics. These might include persons likely to be particularly knowledgeable, influential, or otherwise key to understanding the situation. This 'theoretical sampling' involves selecting those who will help in testing out or further understanding the emerging theory.

In situations where it is difficult to get hold of participants, perhaps because the topic is sensitive, 'snowball' sampling can be used. Having got hold of one relevant person and, say, interviewed them, you ask if they know of others who could be interviewed on the topic. And so on . . .

Market researchers and political pollsters often use quota samples. This approach depends on a knowledge of the characteristics of the population of interest. Perhaps the relative proportions of persons in different socio-economic groupings, gender ratios, etc. The researcher's task is to get hold of quotas with different characteristics. If done conscientiously, this produces samples which are representative in numbers of those with specific characteristics in the population. A similar approach uses telephone surveys where the results are weighted to correspond to the proportions in the population. Quota samples do not produce fully representative samples in the way that random sampling does. Trawling the high street some afternoon to get your quota of manual labourers, professionals, etc. won't necessarily give you a truly representative picture of the population as a whole.

> 🔹 *The website (www.wiley.com/college/robson) gives links to material on sampling and sample sizes*

Laboratory Research

The practicalities of collecting data are very different for those working in a laboratory and those who have to leave the familiar environment of their college and enter what social researchers call 'the field'. If you are carrying out your research in some type of laboratory, this is, as it were, a home fixture. A major task is to persuade possible participants to enter your territory through flattery, payment, appealing to their altruism, or whatever ethical means are at your disposal.

'Subjects' or 'participants'?

Some laboratory disciplines, for example experimental psychology, have traditionally used the term 'subjects' for those taking part in their research. However, the British Psychological Society (BPS) in their 'Code of Human Research Ethics' notes that it is now common practice to refer to a person serving as a data source for research as a 'participant'. This recognizes their active role, while using 'subject' has been viewed as portraying people as passive recipients. Talking in terms of participating 'serves to acknowledge the autonomy and agency of the individual in contributing to the research, and their right to withdraw at any time' (British Psychological Society, 2010; p. 6).

The BPS recognize that 'subject' still has currency in some contexts, such as 'within-subject designs'. The American Psychological Society stresses the need to be consistent with the traditions of the field in which one is working and now appears to take a more even-handed stance in the participant/ subject debate (American Psychological Association, 2013; p. 73). My advice is to check journals in your field and follow their usage. I use 'participant' in this text, partly because I am seeking to cover many different situations and fields, but also because I find the BPS arguments for its use convincing.

Informed Consent

Participants should know what they are letting themselves in for and give explicit agreement to this. Whether or not a formal consent form should be used depends on the particular circumstances of the study and should be discussed and agreed with your supervisor. Indications favouring the use of formal consent forms include the possibility of stress or distress to those taking part. As discussed in the previous chapter (p. 76) some areas, such as social psychology, have made substantial use of deception in the past. The true purpose of the study is not revealed and a cover story used. The justification for such practices has been that, if informed of the true purpose, participants would have behaved differently in some way. Deception is now relatively rare and you are advised not to use it unless it is explicitly sanctioned by your supervisor (and an ethics committee). If deception is used, participants should be debriefed as to the true purpose of the study afterwards. Establishing whether some of those involved saw through the deception can provide you with useful information.

Box 4.1 gives an example of an informed consent form, Box 4.2 an example of a letter to send to parents if you are planning to carry out a project involving schoolchildren. Specific details will obviously depend on the project. Projects involving children should also get the children's informed consent – using a form where the language is appropriate to the age and ability of the children taking part.

Box 4.1 Example of a simple 'Informed consent' form

[Use headed paper from your department. *Get permission to do this – your supervisor should help*. The address and contact details (including how to contact you by phone or e-mail) are needed].

[TITLE OF PROJECT]

[Name of Researcher]:

1. I confirm that I have read the information sheet for the above study, understand what it says and have asked any questions I have about the study.

2. I agree to be interviewed in a one-to-one discussion that will be audio-recorded, transcribed anonymously and used for the purposes of research.

3. I understand that the audio-recording of the interview will be stored securely and only used for publishing the results of the research.

4. I understand that my participation is voluntary and that I am free to withdraw at any time either before or during the research interview and during a two-week cooling-off period following the interview, without giving any reason, and without any services I currently receive, or will receive in the future, being affected.

Name of Participant: Date: Signature:

_____   _____   _____

Name of Researcher: Date: Signature:

_____   _____   _____

Box 4.2 Example of a letter to a parent for a project with schoolchildren

[Use headed paper from your department. *Get permission to do this – your supervisor should help*. The address and contact details (including how to contact you by phone or e-mail) are needed.]

Dear [Name of Parent or Guardian]

Re: **[TITLE OF PROJECT]**

My name is [   ] and I am in the final year of a degree course in [give details]. I am doing a project about [give details] and would really appreciate your help by allowing me to talk to your son or daughter about this.

I have planned to talk to each pupil who takes part for up to [give details of time]. I will record the interview to help me remember what they have said and to help in writing a report. The interviews will be confidential and no one will be named in the report.

If you are happy for your son or daughter to take part, I should be very grateful if you would sign the attached form and return it to school.

If you would like to know more about the project, please contact me at the above address.

Many thanks for taking the time to read this letter.

Yours sincerely

The website (www.wiley.com/college/robson) gives links to material on informed consent and anonymity

Gaining Access

Research outside the laboratory is an away fixture, out in the big wide world. In this situation, gaining access can be a problem. The difficulty varies widely from setting to setting, and appears to be getting more problematic. Worries about paedophiles can make studies involving the observation of children sensitive. The management of commercial centres such as shopping malls are likely to be wary of anyone pestering their customers and getting in the way of their buying things.

Just as you can take it as a good working assumption that all research involving people may have ethical implications, the basic rule is that you need formal permission to carry out your research study in any private setting. The same applies in any environment, such as a school or hospital, where there is not totally open access. For some types of organization, this formal permission has to be granted before there is a direct approach to a specific institution. For example, a large business could require head office approval before one of their plants is approached. For others, you simply contact an organization directly. Again, as with ethical considerations, you should receive advice and support from your supervisor.

Box 4.3 Seeking access – ways of making contact

☐ *Help from supervisor.* If your supervisor has suggested you seek access to a particular organization where she has links, it is reasonable to expect that she will make the initial contact for you and possibly set up a meeting. Subsequent contacts are up to you. In other cases, a supervisor should give you advice but the contact is likely to be your responsibility

☐ *Use of family or friends.* Often the best and most trouble-free route. In fact it is not uncommon for the selection of a topic to be heavily influenced by the knowledge that a family member has good links with a firm or other organization that is likely to be favourably disposed to your involvement with the place.

☐ *Your previous contact or involvement.* Also an excellent route, providing that the involvement was positive on both sides. This may be where the stint you did as a volunteer with a charity, or wherever, pays dividends. If you had, or continue to have, an insider role in the organization then your project could be of career benefit.

☐ *Cold calling. If it is the only way.* Take any advice you can get about the places to approach and who to contact ('School X seems open and friendly but I would keep away from Y'). A phone call where you try to interest someone in your project is probably best. You could try a letter but making that your initial contact is a very risky strategy.

Finding the place to carry out your project

As with other aspects of doing your project, finding the right organization is either straightforward and almost self-evident, or calls for a lot of effort. Box 4.3 lists some of the ways in which you might go about this task if it isn't obvious. Note the warning to avoid just writing cold without prior informal contact. Your letter could sit in someone's in-tray before being binned, or it could do a tour around the organization with nobody viewing it as their responsibility.

Making the contact

Personal contact is more likely to get a result than using a letter, but it is also important to get things in writing. If anything goes wrong, this can be a valuable safeguard. It's not unknown for a manager to try to wriggle out of a tricky situation by claiming that you were doing something that wasn't previously agreed.

On a more positive note, establishing a link when seeking access may lead to the person being interested in what you are doing and facilitating your involvement. It may even be that through discussion you can refocus your study to cover aspects that the firm or organization would find of direct value. If this is the case, they will be keen to facilitate your work.

More generally, you should beware of just using the organization, or other setting which is letting you have access, as 'research-fodder'. They could legitimately feel that they were being used just to help you get a degree. This feeling could inoculate them from any further involvement with research. Your aim should be to leave them at least as favourably disposed to research as when you started – preferably more so.

A good rule is that participants should get something out of the experience. At a minimum this should be an offer by you to let them see your report, preferably in a form which is written to communicate with them (which is unlikely to be in the same format as the report needed for your course). This is something which could be written into any contract you enter into with your hosts (see following section). In some situations, it may be appropriate for you to agree to provide recommendations for improvement or change. You could also offer to give a presentation to those who have taken part in your research. They often have considerable interest in the views of an outsider such as yourself into what is going on.

Box 4.4 summarizes the things you need to have on your agenda when making contact with a view to gaining access.

The process of obtaining formal approval can take a long time. Doing research in some settings will require clearance by a body outside the actual place in which you hope to work. Perhaps they require police checks to establish that you don't have a criminal record, which can take months. The message is that, as soon as it becomes clear that you would like to carry out the research in a particular setting, and you know the broad outlines of what you propose to do, start the process of gaining access. Don't wait until you have completed all your preparations and want to start the next week.

Formal approval isn't enough

Clearing the hurdle of formal approval doesn't necessarily mean that you are going to be welcomed in the organization, classroom, ward, shop-floor or wherever. The people who you hope will participate may be suspicious of you and of your motives. If there is a history of bad relations with management, or they are under stress, or facing threats of change or closure, you are unlikely to get cooperation. You may well be viewed as a management stooge. If your study has, or might appear to have, an evaluative

Box 4.4 Seeking access – approach strategies

Assuming that, one way or another, you know which organization to target and, preferably, have the name or position of a contact (if not, get advice on this, probably from your supervisor):

☐ Phone them and try to arrange a face-to-face session. Who you are, where you are from and (very briefly) what you hope to do – and why. If they want to know, say what it would involve for them. Unless you get a totally negative response, ask if you can come and see them and explain in more detail. Arrange a date and time.

☐ Send a letter or e-mail thanking the person for their time and confirming the meeting. It can be a good idea to include a sheet giving an outline of your project and the purpose of your involvement (otherwise give it out at the meeting).

☐ At the meeting discuss this outline. Be flexible if some aspects concern them. Ask if there are things which they find valuable or interesting which can be emphasized. Offer to provide feedback in the form of a report or otherwise. Be limited in what you ask for. If things go well when you are there, it won't be difficult to do more. If things go badly you may be glad to escape.

☐ Some organizations insist on a formal contract (see below). If not, it is a good idea to send a letter or e-mail next day thanking them and outlining what you think was agreed. Perhaps with a note saying that if you haven't heard from them by . . . , you will take it that they agree, and that you look forward to seeing them on Monday next, 2nd November at 9 a.m. — or whenever. Shortly before that date, ring to confirm when you will arrive. Don't be upset if a receptionist denies any knowledge of the arrangement on that date; just show them the letter.

dimension, word is likely to get out that you are checking on their performance in some way, with the possibility of dire consequences for them – and for your relationship.

It is important that you find ways of getting over to all those likely to be involved what you are doing and why. And, of course, that your motives are pure, and there is no hidden agenda (see discussion on ethics, Chapter 3, p. 74). One strategy is to establish a relationship of trust with an influential and popular person in the organization, who will effectively act as your informal sponsor ('He's all right. We can trust him.'). This calls for a certain amount of understanding of the dynamics within the setting, which may take time for you to develop. It is not unknown for someone who occupies a marginal or isolated position to want to chum up with the researcher. This can have the effect of your sharing their position.

Should everyone involved have given their informed consent to taking part? In a study of purchasing patterns in a supermarket, the extent to which you seek informed consent will depend on the exact nature of the study. You don't need consent from shoppers whom you simply observe, possibly through closed circuit TV. If, on the other hand, you interview shoppers about their purchases, they should agree to take part knowing what you are doing, and with an assurance of confidentiality. The default position is that you always need to have considered whether or not informed consent is called for. And if the decision is made that it isn't, justification should be given. At the least, this should have been discussed and agreed with your supervisor. Ethical approval committees will expect a reasoned case for the decision made.

Formal and informal contracts

There is much to be said for preparing, and agreeing, a formal contract with whoever is the responsible person in the organization. They, or your university, may have a standard pro-forma for this. It should specify both the nature of your research and also the access conditions. There will also be agreements about confidentiality and the organization's rights with respect to any report which is produced. Try to get the agreement worded so that they have the right to see and comment on drafts, and possibly add their own comments, but that they can't veto the production of a report.

Such written agreements are valuable in case something goes wrong, or personnel change. If, when you approach the organization, they suggest that it is all fine and they don't want to bother with a formal contract, it is advisable to send them a letter specifying your understanding of what they have agreed to as suggested in Box 4.2.

Approaching participants

It has already been stressed that the default expectation is that participants must give their informed consent to taking part in your project (see p. 86). How you go about getting the consent depends very much on the type of project. In a laboratory experiment or other study you have, perhaps, advertised for participants in your university department or generally in the institution, or in the community. Anyone who indicates an interest

---

Box 4.5 Participant information sheet

[Use headed paper from your department. *Get permission to do this – your supervisor should help*. The address and contact details (including how to contact your by phone or e-mail) are needed.]

☐ Introduce yourself. I am a student at . . . . working on a final-year research project on . . . . I hope that you will be prepared to take part.

☐ Explain what will be involved. Give details about their involvement (e.g. fill in a questionnaire; be interviewed on . . . . occasions; take part in a focus group). Stress that their involvement will be strictly confidential and on an anonymous basis. Make it clear that, if they agree to take part, they can change their mind at any time.

☐ What do they do next? Tell them how they let you know that they are willing to take part (e.g. tear-off slip on bottom of the sheet using stamped addressed envelope supplied). Give them time to think about this. Ask them to contact you if they have questions.

---

should get a letter, e-mail, or phone call explaining what would be involved. In a survey, the first step might be a letter to people who fit the requirements of your study. In field-based projects, seeking and getting agreement to work in the organization or wherever precedes contacting possible individual participants. The process of getting their informed consent may be started on an individual basis or through group meetings.

Box 4.5 gives suggestions for the approach to take in an information sheet for participants. If you plan to contact anyone by phone, you should have sent out a letter introducing yourself and the project, saying you plan to phone about their taking part. A possibility is providing a return slip where they tick a box indicating that they wish (or don't wish) to be involved. With some projects this could all be dealt with by e-mail (no need for stamped addressed envelopes).

It is a good idea to prepare a checklist of the topics you want to cover, including those on the information sheet. Pilot it by arranging to phone a colleague and getting feedback on how it came over, particularly if you find it stressful. Remind possible participants about the letter you sent. Give some thought to the best time of day to make the call given their situation. In organizations, a receptionist should be able to advise.

Getting on and getting out

Getting on in the place where you are doing your project can be very straightforward, or almost impossible, and anywhere in between. There's no rule against enjoying yourself, providing this doesn't get in the way of your research role. If you land in a situation which you find stressful, you need help. You can, for example, find yourself torn between groups with different interests who seek to recruit you to their view of problems or difficulties. Your support network should be in place before you get into the research situation. This can be your supervisor by phone, or available for texting, or e-mailing. Or a colleague, or group of colleagues, with whom you can have informal discussion sessions either via phone or text, or face-to-face (see Chapter 1, p. 13 on support groups).

Suppose that you come across a situation where you suspect, or are told, that something illegal or unethical is taking place. Perhaps there is some fiddle going on where employees are falsifying expense accounts. Or so-called care staff are mistreating confused old people in a residential home. This is where you definitely need advice and support. You must discuss this with your supervisor, who should advise you about the appropriate action to be taken – and about who should take the action (see the sections on ethics in Chapter 3, p. 74).

As a novice researcher, you should not be carrying out your research in a situation where there appears to be a chance that your safety, or health, is at risk. Possible risks include physical threat or abuse, or psychological trauma resulting from any such threats or abuse, or from your experiences while carrying out the research. You might be put in a compromising situation leading to you being accused of behaving improperly. Again, this is an issue to be discussed with your supervisor.

The website (www.wiley.com/college/robson) gives links to material on safety issues

Just as it can be difficult to make the transition between preparation for the project and data collection, it can be hard to extricate yourself from the research setting. You can usually persuade yourself that staying on for a bit longer will yield valuable data. The task of analysing and interpreting the data, and writing the report, can be avoided for a little longer. Usually, harsh practicalities take over. If you don't leave now, you will never complete by the deadline when reports have to be submitted.

This is best handled by deciding, before you start the main data collection, the date by which you must pull out. Make this part of your formal or informal contract with the organization or institution. And make sure that everyone knows this. It can often be valuable to factor in a return visit, at a date pretty close to the time by which you have to complete. The visit can be used for feedback to the participants (although, if pushed, that could be at a later date after the deadline). It may also give you additional information on how things have changed or developed since you left, and perhaps give you the opportunity to try out with them some of your findings and interpretations.

Insider research

Insider research is research carried out by someone who, prior to the study, already has some role or position in the setting or organization which is the focus of the research. For an undergraduate research project, this would be most likely to be carried out by a practitioner, such as a teacher or social worker, currently following a degree programme whether on a full-time or part-time basis.

Focusing the project on your work setting has several attractions. You will have both formal and informal knowledge about the place where you work, helping you to avoid pitfalls that an outsider might not. In some cases, it is an explicit requirement, or at least an expectation, that you will carry out something likely to be of value to the service which is supporting your involvement with the course. Having done a project which is seen as valuable by colleagues and managers will stand you in good stead in your future career.

Other possibilities include linking the project to an involvement you have with, say, church or youth work, sports or athletics clubs, choirs, orchestras, or student union activities, including support services. A former student of mine was a keen surfer and set up a project on 'surf bunnies', female members of her surfing group. Unfortunately the lure of the surf proved too strong and her project was never completed, which is one danger of following up something you are keenly interested in.

While insider research has many attractions, it has its difficulties. The fact that you already have some role in the setting, distinct from that of researcher, will cause complications. Interviewing colleagues can be fraught with status issues. If you have a relatively lowly position, then managers may not be forthcoming. If high, then the workers will watch what they say.

Insider research seems particularly prone to raising ethical issues. Suppose that you hear or discover something with your researcher hat on which reveals questionable practices. You should seek to anticipate likely problems and to have made it clear to participants that, while you will normally respect confidentiality, there are limits in relation to acts such as client abuse and other clearly illegal activities. Again, as discussed earlier, you should expect to receive advice and support on any such matters from your supervisor and support network of colleagues.

📁 *The website (www.wiley.com/college/robson) gives links to material on anticipating problems*

Pilots

In fixed design research, piloting is a crucial part of the process. Ideally, this style of research calls for the main data collection exercise to go like clockwork. You have a detailed plan worked out in advance and the task is to put that plan into operation. We don't live in an ideal world, and things may crop up which force you to modify your plans (the most common scenario being that you realize you won't be able to do everything you planned to – which is why you should give some thought to a Plan B – a 'traded down' design which will at least give you something to analyse and discuss – see p. 99).

Running pilot studies is the main way of reality-testing your proposals and fine-tuning your plan. This involves trying out all aspects of the data collection on a small scale. The specific details vary from one project to another but typically you pilot using a small sample selected in the same way as is proposed for the main exercise. You have to ensure that the main exercise won't be contaminated by your pilot work (e.g. so that you're not in danger of selecting some of the same participants; or that details aren't passed on from those in the pilot to later participants). Pre-testing of all procedures should take place in the pilot work. Are there problems in understanding questions or instructions? Are tasks too easy or too difficult? Debriefing of pilot participants, to find out any problems or issues from their perspective, can be very illuminating.

Pilot work should extend, beyond data collection aspects, to piloting what you plan to do with the data subsequently. It can be helpful to use the pilot data as a basis for generating some dummy data as if from a similar number of participants as you expect to have in the main data collection exercise. You then use this data to test out whether you know what to do to carry out your proposed basic data analyses.

When the pilot work throws up problems, they have to be addressed before you proceed. If these are major – say, several of the pilot participants misunderstand instructions – then, if at all possible, do some further pilot work before moving to the main data collection.

Flexible design research is more forgiving. The details of what you are doing in, say, a case study, can and should be sorted out as you feel your way through, gaining access and establishing trust with those involved. A rather different form of piloting may well be needed if you are a novice researcher. Some prior development of the researcher skills that the project calls for will help you feel more confident when interacting with participants. For example, some sessions of participant observation in settings similar to the one in your project can be confidence boosting.

Collecting the Data

Your pilot work should have given you the chance of testing out the way you are going about the task of data collection. Obviously, the specific details of this task vary from one data collection method to another but the general question you should ask yourself is: 'What is the simplest and easiest way that I can collect the data that I need to get answers to the research questions?' Just because you have the possibility of, say, videotaping sessions, doesn't mean that you necessarily have to do so.

For many projects, audio recording is a preferred option, particularly when using semi-structured interviews. Work out in advance what you are going to do with the recordings. Do you need to transcribe them all? Or will it be sufficient to replay them and make notes, perhaps with selective transcription of relevant responses?

Whatever equipment you use, it is crucial you know how to operate it. If you are recording, get hold of the best-quality equipment you can find and make sure when piloting that the microphone picks up voices satisfactorily. Make sure that you have any necessary spares, particularly new, fully-charged batteries. Train yourself to keep an eye on when you are low on recording space so that you don't miss the last minutes of an interview.

You need a system. Prepare a list of what you have to do. Things like: phone to confirm just before the visit you arranged; check any equipment is in working order before visit, spare batteries, etc.; check equipment set up and working; label copies of recordings, notes, files, etc. Sort this out when piloting, making sure you include everything important.

Remember that you not only need to time-budget the actual data collection, but also the time and resources you need once you have the data. It doesn't make sense to have all these lovely data if you haven't got the time to get as much as you can out of them. The process of analysis and interpretation of the data is covered in the next chapter.

What to Do if You Run into Difficulties or Out of Time

If the agreed departure date is looming without your having completed all you had hoped and planned to do, a swift review of the situation is called for.

It is important that you give yourself sufficient time both to analyse and interpret the data that you do have, and also to make the most of it in your report. What you don't do is to stick doggedly to the original data collection plan. There are no prizes for having reams of unanalysed data and no report.

It is highly advisable to have given some thought to Plan B before you get into this position. That is, a slimmed-down version of the research with, perhaps, fewer interviews or only studying one site rather than three, or whatever. Something which, barring an absolute disaster, you are confident you can complete. If you are in difficulty, focus on this slimmed-down version, and regard anything else you complete as a bonus, which you might be able to stitch in somehow.

Lots of things can go wrong and some probably will. Participants may decide that they want out. People's personal circumstances change and they may not wish to continue. If a few withdraw, this shouldn't be a problem. In surveys, you should have a procedure for selecting replacements. In flexible designs, you can usually deal with this by finding someone else who is willing to help, though it can be a real problem if the person opting out is one of the key persons in the situation. If many people want to withdraw, then this is likely to be symptomatic of a serious problem, which may be specific to the research or indicative of a wider malaise. Either way, seek advice from your supervisor. You might have to start again in another setting unless the root of the problem can be dealt with.

You may run into design difficulties. Perhaps you find that a randomization process, say, the random allocation of participants to experimental or control groups, hasn't worked properly. It's not unknown for someone you relied on to do this deciding that it would be better if certain people were in the experimental group and fiddling the allocation. The moral is to keep such aspects under your control. However, if a design breakdown does occur, it may well be that you have to live with the situation. Providing that you give an honest account of what happened, and take into consideration the changed situation when analysing and interpreting the data, you should be able to rescue the situation.

Don't despair even with the absolute disaster situation. Unless it's your total incompetence or general lack of ability to organize (which I'm sure it isn't), something must have happened externally to lead to the disaster. With ingenuity, you ought to be able to make something of this. Remember, what you need to produce is a well-written, professionally-presented report which gives data-driven answers to a set of research questions. There is no iron rule which says these must be the questions you initially planned to answer. If disaster has struck, you are, however, likely to be light on data. An account of your journey from initial to final questions is helpful not only in legitimately bulking up your report but also in demonstrating your ability to retrieve a difficult situation.

Further Reading

Daniel, J. (2012). Sampling essentials: Practical guidelines for making sampling choices. Thousand Oaks, CA.: Sage.

Thorough, non-technical coverage of how to select sample type and size.

Howard, K., Sharp, J.A., & Peters, J. (2002). *The management of a student research project.* (3rd ed.). Aldershot: Gower.

Gives suggestions on what you need to consider to complete the project. Very useful if you have a complicated project and/or are not good at organization.

Knight, P.T. (2002). Small-scale research: Pragmatic inquiry in social science and the caring professions. London: Sage.

Section on 'Doing it' (pp. 161–172) covers likely mishaps and a full range of other practical issues.

Chapter 4 Tasks

1 *Work out a project schedule*. The schedule should include:

☐ a list of all the things you need to do up to and including handing in your completed project report
☐ the sequence in which they have to be done, and
☐ your estimate of the time each will take.

A good way of doing this is to draw a chart where each task takes up one row (see the examples below). Dates run along the top with the expected time for the task being represented by a horizontal bar with the left end at the expected start date and the right the estimated completion date. Tasks can run in sequence, in parallel or overlap. Keep tasks to a manageable number (say up to 20) so you can fit the chart on a single page. The examples are just word-processed tables. Versions known as Gantt charts can be produced easily using specialist software.

🏛 *The website (www.wiley.com/college/robson) gives links to material on anticipating problems*

Try to fill in the chart now with your best estimate of the time the various aspects will take. You may need to revise this when you have read the next two chapters and have a clearer idea of what is likely to be involved in analysing your data and writing the report.

When you are actually collecting data you will need to prepare a blank version of the chart and:

☐ *Fill in the bars* as the project proceeds.

☐ *Keep it up to date*. If a task takes longer than anticipated, extend the time line to the right. If you start one late, show this on the chart, and

☐ *Take emergency action* if it looks as if delays threaten you not being able to complete by the deadlines (see 'What to do if you run into difficulties or out of time', p. 98).

2. *Work out your Plan B*. What bits of your original plan could you jettison in an emergency? What is the minimum in terms of sample size, number of settings visited, persons interviewed, amount of time in the setting, etc. which will give sufficient information to be able to get at least some kind of answer to your main research question?

Examples of project schedule

1. Fixed design project	June	July	Aug	Sept	Oct	Nov	Dec	Jan	Feb	Mar	Apr	May
Deciding project focus	—											
Design decisions (approach, methods, research questions)		—										
Reading, library and internet searching	—											
Ethics committee deadline				14th								
Negotiate access	—											
Write questionnaire	—											
Pilot questionnaire	–											
Revise questionnaire	–											
Main data collection	–											
Data analysis	–											
Write report sections (literature review, methodology, analysis)		—										
Write full first draft of report	—											
Seminar presentation											14th	
Draft to supervisor											30th	
Produce final version of report	—											
Completion deadline												21st

2. Flexible design project

2. Flexible design project	June	July	Aug	Sept	Oct	Nov	Dec	Jan	Feb	Mar	Apr	May
Deciding project focus	—											
Design decisions (approach, methods, research questions)		—										
Reading, library and internet searching		—										
Ethics committee deadline				14th								
Negotiate access	—											
Data collection		—										
Data analysis		—										
Write report sections (literature review, methodology, analysis)		—										
Write full first draft of report		—										
Seminar presentation											14th	
Draft to supervisor											30th	
Produce final version of report		—										
Completion deadline												21st

Notes:

These are examples; tailor your chart to the particular circumstances of your project.
They assume that work on the project is started in June of one academic year and continues throughout the next one.

Part III

Making Something of It

Collecting data almost inevitably depends on your getting active cooperation from others, particularly the people participating in your interviews, filling in your questionnaires, etc. However, once you have those data, making something of them is very much up to you. This can come as a relief. It is something you can get stuck into, without having to rely on the vagaries of others.

Nevertheless it is sensible to seek advice, particularly if you have substantial amounts of quantitative data, which might require statistical treatment. Or, for that matter, substantial amounts of qualitative data, when it may be helpful to use a software package for analysis. While all researchers, even first-time ones, are expected to carry out a competent analysis of their data, it is now widely accepted that the skill called for in this area is more that of knowing how to get advice from a data analysis expert, than being such an expert in your own right (however, as always, check what the expectations and regulations are for your course).[*]

Recall also, as discussed in Chapter 4, p. 97, that data analysis should be part of piloting the design of your study. It is an aspect of the so-called 'Sod's law' (known in more polite circles as the 'law of maximum perversity') that, if you haven't considered how your data are to be analysed in advance of their collection, you end up with something that is an unanalysable mish-mash. Don't test the applicability of this law.

---

[*] If you are expected to carry out data analysis and interpretation without expert assistance (beyond assistance from your supervisor) your course programme will normally have provided appropriate taught courses). The material in this chapter can be regarded as revision, in similar fashion to that provided in Chapter 2 and the links for Chapter 2 in the student website, www.wiley.com/college/robson.

In fixed designs, the main data analysis takes place as a separate and distinctive phase after you have completed the main data collection exercise. If you have done prior piloting, it has already been pointed out that it is a good idea to do an earlier analysis of the results, partly to draw as many lessons as possible from it, but also so that you can try out the analysis itself (perhaps using dummy data based on the data from the pilot).

In flexible designs, analysis is much more intermingled with the data collection process. Some analysis of the initial data is needed to help guide later data collection. This does not preclude later and more extensive analysis, after the main collection is completed.

You should, if at all possible, build in a little leeway in your time-planning so that if something previously unexpected arises from the data analysis, there is an opportunity to return to the setting where you have been collecting data to check it out in some way.

5

Analysing and Interpreting Your Findings

All data analysis can also be considered as a process of interpretation, of dealing with the 'raw' data in such ways that the messages contained within it become clear. However, having done this to the best of your ability, you need to take an overview of what you have found. This overall interpretation forms the concluding section of the chapter.

What This Chapter Tries to Do

This chapter does not try to provide a comprehensive coverage of all aspects of data analysis. That would call for a much longer book solely devoted to the topic. The section in the chapter on quantitative analysis concentrates on simple ways of describing, summarizing and displaying quantitative data. It makes no attempt (beyond giving references at the end of the chapter and material on the website, www.wiley.com/college/robson.) to cover complex statistical analyses as called for by those working in some disciplines. However, my experience is that students in these fields not uncommonly make a poor job of the simpler aspects of data analysis. So, I hope that reminders will not go amiss.

For those without a strong statistical background, I hope that you get the message that a perfectly adequate treatment of numerical data can often be achieved by summary statistics and clear displays. Even in projects with predominantly qualitative data, there are usually some numbers around which, simply but adequately dealt with, can enhance the overall analysis.

In a similar manner, the treatment of qualitative data analysis in the chapter makes no attempt to provide coverage of the many and varied approaches that are current (though, again there are references at the end of the chapter and material on the website). Some general features of qualitative data analysis common to several specific approaches are summarized as an introduction to those unfamiliar with the field. This is followed by coverage of the widely-used grounded theory approach to help you appreciate what is involved.

If your project is largely quantitative, the following section should provide pointers to the treatment of any qualitative data that you have collected, including those from a second, subsidiary, method.

Preparing for Analysis

The first step is to know, in some detail, exactly what data you have. The second is to make sure you have them in an easily accessible form. This is the stage when the systematic researcher comes into their own, and the disorganized one suffers.

With fixed designs, you will have decided at the design stage what data you are going to collect so you should know what to expect. The decision about the main way in which you are going to analyse these data should also have been made then. If things haven't worked out quite as you anticipated, say if one or more of the sites where you were going to collect data pulls out at a late stage, which forces changes, then you are going to have to do the best with the data you have. Don't worry. You can almost always make something of partial data.

If you have followed the advice to devote a little time and effort to using a second, subsidiary, type of data collection, the results from this can be dealt with in a more open-ended manner. Essentially, you explore what you have got and see if it helps throw light on the findings from your main data analysis.

With flexible designs, you won't know in advance exactly what data, either in amount or type, you will obtain. Also, your research questions may change, depending to a considerable extent on how things develop when doing your fieldwork. This makes it difficult to decide on the relevance of the various things that you have collected. Don't assume that simply because you have collected some data that they have to be analysed. Researchers are only human. They find it difficult to jettison some aspect that they were keen on, particularly if they had to overcome problems in getting hold of the data, even when there appears to be little relevance to the questions they seek to answer. Once you realize that you are going down a blind alley in relation to how you now view your research questions, you will have to cut your losses and move on to pursuing things of greater relevance. However, it's almost inevitable that you end up with some unusable data. It might be possible to 'tweak' your research questions so the data become usable – but beware of the 'drunkard and lamppost situation' (looking for a dropped watch under the lamp even though it was dropped somewhere else). Put it down to experience.

Quantitative (Numerical) Data

Data often either come as numbers, or can be converted into numbers. Virtually all fixed designs, particularly experiments and surveys, yield such numerical data, but there are almost always some data of this type in a research project.

A good thing about quantitative data is that there are commonly agreed rules about how they should be dealt with. A bad thing, for the novice, is that the statistical analysis of quantitative data can become very complex. For the small-scale project on which this book focuses, there is often little need for complex statistical analysis. One exception is where you are focusing on a topic suggested by your supervisor which builds on previous work using complex analyses. These analyses then provide a model that you can follow.

The priority is to summarize and display your numerical data. Even in a small project, it is easy to end up with strings of numbers where it is very difficult to see the wood for the trees.

The following sections cover commonly occurring types of quantitative data showing how they can be dealt with. They are illustrated by focusing on the demographic or 'background information' questions used to find out about the personal characteristics of respondents in many projects. However, the treatment is the same wherever the data come from.

Categorical variables

One type of quantitative data is the number of responses that fall within different categories.

Situation 1: Responses fall into one or other of two categories. Example: *The sex question.* Respondents are asked to tick a box indicating whether they are male or female.[*]

The kinds of analysis you can do include calculating the numbers falling in each category, and the relative proportions in the two categories (e.g. 60% male, 40% female). Appropriate types of statistical tests for this kind of data are discussed on p. 120. In analysing the results of surveys, this type of data is sometimes coded (e.g. females are coded '1' and males '0'). The code numbers assigned are conventional and arbitrary (they could be females coded '0' and males '1' – or indeed any numbers you like).

---

[*] There is often confusion between 'gender' and 'sex'. A widely accepted usage follows that of the World Health Organization where 'sex' refers to the biological characteristics that define men and women, while 'gender' refers to socially constructed roles, behaviour, etc. Hence, 'male' and 'female' are sex categories. 'Masculine' and 'feminine' are gender categories.

Situation 2: Responses fall into one of several different categories. Example: *Current marital status.* The question might be:

What is your current marital status? Please tick one of the boxes:

Married ☐   Widowed ☐   Divorced ☐   Separated ☐   Never married ☐

(There are complexities here which have to be thought about and instructions provided. For example, does 'marriage' include civil partnerships, same sex partnerships or marriages, or cohabiting couples? Where does an annulment fit in?)

The same limited range of analyses is possible. Any coding is again arbitrary.

Ordered categorical variables

Situation 3: Responses fall into one of several different ordered categories. Example: *Degree level performance.* In the UK it has been traditional to award first degrees in different 'classes', and the question might be:

What class of degree did you obtain? Please tick one of the boxes:

First ☐   Upper ☐   Lower ☐   Third ☐   Unclassified ☐
        second   second   (pass degree)

This is a further situation where a response falls into one of several different categories. However, the variable 'class of degree' can be ordered (i.e. a first class degree is at a higher level than an upper second, which is in turn higher than a lower second, etc.).

The same kinds of analysis are possible as in the two previous situations. There are also statistical tests known as non-parametric tests which can be used with categorical data.

Example: *Satisfaction ratings.* The same kind of data result from a commonly used 'satisfaction' question, e.g.:

How do you rate your experience of the course so far? Please circle one:

Excellent   Very good   Good   Satisfactory   Poor   Very poor   Awful

This question can, of course, be asked in many ways with different labels for the categories. Common to each of them is the idea that the responses can be ordered to indicate level of satisfaction. However, while the answers are often coded numerically (say, Excellent = 7; Very good = 6; Good = 5: Satisfactory = 4; Poor = 3; Very poor = 2; Awful = 1) any such numbers are pretty much arbitrary and should be treated with caution. One difficulty is that we don't know the relative differences between the categories, only their order. Using numbers for the categories can mislead you into thinking that, say, a '6' represents twice the satisfaction of a '3'. More generally, any kind of arithmetical operation, such as working out, or comparing, average ratings of satisfaction (see below) is suspect and to be avoided. However, people who should know better often do this (you will see average ratings of this kind quoted in published journal articles).

Summarizing and displaying categorical data

The data can be displayed in the form of a table or bar chart as illustrated in Table 5.1 and Figure 5.1. The same data are presented in the table and the figure. For small amounts of data, there is not much to choose between the two. A figure, particularly with more complex or extensive data, probably communicates better to more audiences. The bar chart shown in Figure 5.1

Table 5.1 Class of degree obtained by respondents

Class of degree	First	Upper second	Lower second	Third	Unclassified
Frequency (number with class of degree)	4	18	12	3	3

Figure 5.1 Class of degree obtained by respondents

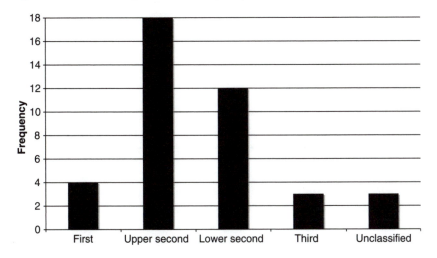

Table 5.2 Comparison of male and female main reasons for choice of university

Frequency (number giving that reason)

Main reason for choice	Females	Males
Low cost of living	3	4
Nearness to home	25	7
Not near to home	0	13
Recommendation by friend	67	12
Recommendation by parent	12	5
Recommendation by school	15	22
Recommendation in a 'good university' guide or newspaper feature	19	39
Reputation for research	0	0
Reputation for teaching	4	0
University brochure or other advertising	93	103
Total	**238**	**205**

Within sex percentages

Main reason for choice	Females (%)	Males (%)
Low cost of living	1.3	2.0
Nearness to home	10.5	3.4
Not near to home	0.0	6.3
Recommendation by friend	28.2	5.9
Recommendation by parent	5.0	2.4
Recommendation by school	6.3	10.7
Recommendation in a 'good university' guide or newspaper feature	8.0	19.0
Reputation for research	0.0	0.0
Reputation for teaching	1.7	0.0
University brochure or other advertising	39.1	50.2
Total	**100**	**100**

is often used to display this kind of data, but there are many alternatives which software such as Excel can easily generate.

More complex displays can be produced by combining the responses from two or more questions or other sources of data. Table 5.2 combines

Figure 5.2 Comparison of male and female main reasons for choice of university

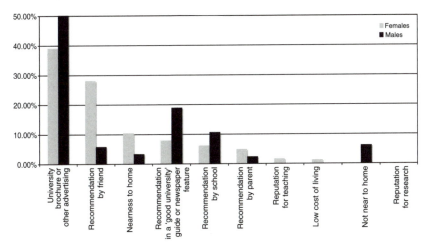

data from a gender question and a 'main reason for choice of university' question. This is known as a cross-tabulation (sometimes as cross-classification). The table presents a cross-tabulation of the two category sex response (male/female) and responses made when students at a sixth form college were asked to give their main reason for choice of university from a list of alternatives. The first part of the table shows the numbers of males and females giving each of the alternatives as their main reason (these are called frequency counts). Statistical packages will produce such tables and also provide row and column totals and percentages. Percentages often show more clearly the pattern of results but you need to think carefully about what you want to know (and show). Here it probably makes more sense to display the distribution of reasons within sexes, i.e. the column percentages, as in the lower part of the table (for example 25 of the 238 females, or 10.5%, give 'Nearness to home' as their main reason). This same information is displayed in Figure 5.2. Note that the ordering of the reasons along the horizontal axis has been arranged with the most popular reasons on the left and the least popular on the right (ordering done on the basis of the female percentages – male percentages could have been used to sort out the order). This, perhaps, makes it somewhat easier to take in the information about the relative popularity of different reasons and of male/female differences. This change of order can be done because the original ordering of reasons as in Table 5.1 was arbitrary.

EXCEL, SPSS and other packages can also give the results of various statistical tests. The most commonly used in the situation shown in Table 5.2 is called Chi-square (χ^2). This provides a measure of the overall difference between the male and female distributions of reasons (in general terms the difference in row frequencies for the two columns). The larger the value of Chi-square the bigger the difference in male and female opinions. This is a useful way of summarizing in a single figure much information about the data. Statistical packages can also provide a value for the statistical significance of the Chi-square value obtained (see below, p. 118). Chi-square can be legitimately calculated for all categorical data, whether or not we are dealing with ordered categories.

Continuous variables

When you are measuring something that can, in principle, take on any value (examples are height, weight and age), this is known as a continuous or measured variable.

Situation: Responses can take on any value. Example: *the age question.* The question can be asked in different ways. For example, directly:

How old are you? ☐ years

or

What is your date of birth? | dd / mm / yy |

With this type of data you can carry out a range of analyses which are not feasible with categorical data.

When the age question is thought likely to be sensitive it might be put in terms of age groups:

What age group are you? Please tick one of the boxes:

Under 20 ☐   20–29 ☐   30–39 ☐   40–49 ☐   50–59 ☐   60 or ☐ above

Asking the question in this way produces data in ordered categories ('twenty-year-olds', 'thirty-year-olds', etc.). Continuous data can always be turned into ordered categorical data and this can be a useful way of summarizing and displaying large amounts of such material.

Calculating summary statistics with continuous variables

The most common type of summary statistic, and one of the most useful, is the simple average, known technically as the arithmetic mean. The idea of an average is well understood and communicates well. There are other ways of getting at what statisticians call the 'central tendency' of a set of figures which can be useful in particular circumstances (see below).

A second main way in which sets of numbers differ from each other is in the amount of variability or spread that they show. Two sets of figures can have the same average, but one might be tightly clustered about a central figure, while the other might be much more dispersed. There are various statistics which capture this aspect, including the range, standard deviation, and variance.

Once you have captured these two features of sets of numbers, you have a very useful short summary of their main characteristics.

Suppose we ask the 'age' question directly or by asking for dates of birth. Responses from 20 participants might be: 17, 20, 20, 20, 21, 22, 23, 23, 24, 24, 24, 24, 24, 25, 25, 26, 28, 30, 31, 45.

As with any data, the way you deal with them depends on what you want to know. Let's say that you're interested in the average age, perhaps to compare this group with some other group or groups. The arithmetic mean – sometimes simply referred to as the mean – is simply obtained by adding all the ages together and dividing by the number of responses:

Mean of the 20 responses = 496/20 = 24.8 years

Asking the age question in the form 'What age range are you in?' stops you from calculating the mean age in this way. You can work out an approximate figure by taking the midpoint of each age group (in the 20–29 group the mid-point lies between 24 and 25, hence 24.5) and multiplying by the number of persons falling within that age group; then adding together the results from the different age groups. When a box like the 'under 20' or '60 and above' is used (which is useful as it ensures that all participants are included), a mid-point has to be guessed – say 15 and 65 respectively.

Here, the estimated mean, if the 20 responses had been entered into the different age range boxes, would be $(15 \times 1) + (24.5 \times 16) + (34.5 \times 2) + (44.5 \times 1)$ divided by 20. This is 520.5/20 = 26.0. Which is an overestimate of the exact average of 24.8 years. A closer estimate would be obtained if you have prior knowledge of the likely age range of the respondents so you could fine-tune the age ranges selected. Here, for example, by using boxes of 'under 20', '20–24', '25–29', '30–34', '35–39' and '40 and over' the corresponding figures would be $(15 \times 1) + (12 \times 22) + (4 \times 27) + (2 \times 32) + (1 \times 47)$ which gives $498/20 = 24.9$. This is one of the many aspects of research for which pilot work is invaluable.

Note that one of the 20 participants is considerably older than the rest, called an 'outlier' by statisticians. Outliers, particularly if they are extreme, can lead to the arithmetic mean being not at all typical of the data.

Where there are extreme outliers, either very low or very high, or the set of scores appears markedly non-normal[†] the *median* can provide a more sensible typical figure. The median is the middle value when a set of numbers is arranged in size order. Or the average of the two middle ones when you have an even number, as here. The median for this set of numbers is 24.[‡]

Calculating variability

The variability or spread of a set of numerical responses to a question or other types of numerical data can be calculated in several ways. For data where the arithmetic mean is appropriate, the corresponding variability statistic is the standard deviation (or variance, which is the standard deviation squared) – see Robson (1994) for details. For anything other than very small amounts of data, this is tedious to calculate and the use of a computer package such as EXCEL or SPSS is recommended.

When the median is appropriate as a measure of central tendency, quartiles are commonly used. Just as the median is the value in the middle of a set of numbers so that half of them are above and half below, the first quartile (Q_1) has a quarter of the numbers below (and three-quarters above) and the third quartile (Q_3) has three quarters below and one quarter above. The measure of variability is the inter-quartile range $(Q_3 - Q_1)$ – or more commonly this is halved to give the semi-inter-quartile range $(Q_3 - Q_1)/2$.

[†] Sets of scores are often close to a so-called 'normal' distribution. This is a particular distribution where, amongst other features, equal numbers of scores are above and below the arithmetic mean, and most of the scores are close to the mean with numbers tapering off as you get further from it.

[‡] The 'mode' is also sometimes used. This is the most commonly occurring value (here 24 which occurs five times). The mode is useful as it can be legitimately used with categorical data. It is whatever category has the highest frequency (i.e. the category with the highest number of responses). In practice it is used mainly when you have large amounts of data.

Table 5.3 Age distribution of participants

Age group	Number of participants
15–19yrs	1
20–24yrs	12
25–29yrs	4
30–34yrs	2
35+ yrs	1

This isn't too difficult to work out by hand, or is straightforward using EXCEL or SPSS.

Displaying continuous variables

There are various ways of displaying the 'age' data. These include a simple table as illustrated in Table 5.3 and Figure 5.3. Note that Table 5.3 is set out differently from Table 5.1 – the latter has the different categories along the top. Table 5.3 presents them down the side. Either can be used. The type of bar chart in Figure 5.3, where the bars are touching, is sometimes known as a histogram, and is conventionally used when, as here, the variable shown (age) is continuous.

Figure 5.3 Age distribution of participants

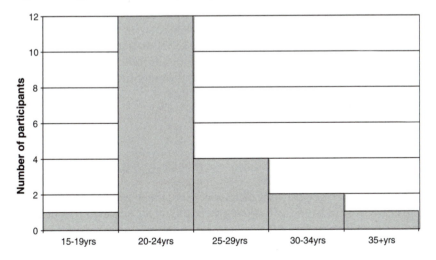

Statistical tests and statistical significance

In projects which generate quantitative data, the answers to research questions often depend on being able to say something about mean scores, commonly about how means differ in different situations or conditions. Statistical tests (more exactly tests of statistical inference) can be used to assess the likelihood that your results could have been obtained, if only chance factors were operating. For example, statistics known as t-tests can be used to assess the probability that a particular mean value differs from zero, or some other predicted or expected value, or of the difference obtained between mean values obtained under two conditions, when only chance factors operate. This is known as assessing the statistical significance of your results. In some areas and disciplines (for example, experimental psychology and medical science), this kind of assessment is considered essential. However, reliance on statistical significance is not recommended because:

☐ Statistical significance is a confusing and unfortunate term. Simply because a result is statistically significant (i.e. unlikely to have happened by chance), says neither that it is significant – in the sense of being important – nor does it tell you directly why the result happened. There can be a whole host of non-chance factors which contribute to the results, depending on the design of your project.

☐ The chance of achieving a statistically significant result increases with the size of your study (i.e. the amount of data you collect). Statistical significance can be virtually guaranteed by carrying out a large enough study. So, paradoxically, a statistically significant result is more likely to be significant (important) if it is obtained in a small study!

☐ The statistical tests used to assess statistical significance make assumptions about the nature of the data collected. In practice, many of these assumptions are often violated, casting doubt on the meaning of the test results. Non-parametric tests have fewer assumptions about the nature of the data but the problem of interpreting statistical significance remains.

Effect sizes

An approach which avoids many of the problems associated with statistical significance is to calculate *effect sizes*. For example, in the situation where a comparison is made between mean scores obtained under two conditions, an effect size can be found by dividing the difference in means by a measure of the variability in the data (the statistic known as Cohen's *d* can be used). Comparisons can then be made between the sizes of effect found in different studies. Results which are not statistically significant can, nevertheless, be important – particularly when they show large effect sizes.

In situations where there is an expectation that you measure statistical significance, it is good practice to also provide effect sizes. This is easy to do when using statistical packages.

Clinical significance

However, even effect sizes do not really tell you much about how significant (in the sense of being meaningful or important) a finding is. This is called *clinical significance* from its use in medical and related settings. At root, it is not an issue which can be determined by statistical analysis. It is a judgment that has to be made by those with an interest in the findings and their use, whether they are consumers, professionals, managers, other researchers, examiners, or whoever.

Your job, as discussed in the following chapter on writing up the research, is to make it clear what your findings are and to present your interpretation of their meaning and implications. You have exactly the same task whether you are dealing with quantitative or qualitative data (as discussed later in this chapter).

What test do I use?

As well as tests for means, there are statistical tests for just about any situation where you are analysing numerical data. The spreadsheet software Microsoft EXCEL can be used for a wide range of tests. Computer packages such as SPSS (http://www-01.ibm.com/software/uk/analytics/spss/) make the task of analysis deceptively easy. Beware! Unless you know what you are doing, it is all too easy to generate impressive looking garbage. Table 5.4 lists some of the more common tests and what they are used for.

Research questions often boil down to asking whether there are differences between things or whether there are relationships between them. For example, in a study of driving behaviour we might be interested in finding out whether there are differences between male and female performance (say, do male drivers take more risks than female drivers?). Another study might focus on whether there is a relationship between number of years of driving experience and the risks taken. Figure 5.4 illustrates how the results of a study might appear.

The display shown is known as a *scatter plot*. It can be seen that there is a tendency for more risks to be taken by those with less experience, fewer risks by those with more experience. Relationships of this type between measures or variables are known as *correlations*. Correlation coefficients provide a

Table 5.4 Choosing an appropriate statistical test

A Research questions about relationships

Categorical data

Two variables
a) categories not ordered: contingency coefficient
b) ordered categories: Kendall rank correlation

More than two variables
a) categories not ordered: discriminant analysis
b) ordered categories: Kendall partial rank
   correlation

Continuous data

Two variables
Pearson product-moment
   correlation

More than two variables
Multiple regression analysis

B Research questions about differences

Categorical data

Two variables
a) categories not ordered
 i) related samples: McNemar test
 ii) independent samples: Chi-square
b) ordered categories
 i) related samples: Wilcoxon test
 ii) independent samples: Mann-Whitney test

More than two variables
a) categories not ordered
i) related samples: Cochran Q test
ii) independent samples: Chi-square
b) ordered categories
i) related samples: Friedman two-way analysis of
   variance
ii) independent samples: Kruskal-Wallis one-way
   analysis of variance

Continuous data

Two variables
i) related samples: t-test
   (correlated samples)
ii) independent samples: t-test
   (independent samples)

More than two variables
Analysis of variance (type of
   analysis depends on
   design)

---

simple and useful way of describing the strength of such relationships. For the data shown, the appropriate correlation coefficient (the 'Pearson product-moment correlation') is computed as −0.65. The minus sign indicates that we have an inverse relationship. High values on one measure (risk) tend to be paired with low values on the other (experience) and vice versa. Correlation coefficients range from +1 to −1, with the mid-point, 0, indicating no relationship. Statistical significance levels can be computed and tell you how likely it is to get the observed coefficient if there is zero correlation between the variables.

Figure 5.4 Scatter plot showing relationship between driving experience and risks taken

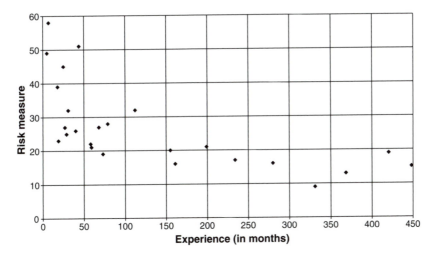

Table 5.4 also lists statistical tests which can be used in more complex designs where you have more than two variables (e.g. in the example above you might have results for several different measures of risk-taking, or you might have measures not only of risk but, say, of driving skill as well).

If you don't already have skills and experience in using statistical tests, you are strongly advised to seek advice from someone who has (unless this is against the regulations). Not every researcher can be expected to be an expert in the analysis of data, and an important skill to be developed as a budding researcher is how and when to use the skills of others.

Do I really need to use statistical tests?

The answer is probably 'yes' if there is a strong expectation in your field of work (and by your supervisor) of using such tests. However, even in such situations, you need to satisfy yourself first that the tests actually add anything to your interpretation of the results, and secondly, whether or not the tests can legitimately be used in the circumstances of your study. You are the one to decide the first issue, but you will probably need advice from someone with statistical expertise for the second one. It is worse to use a statistic incorrectly than not use one at all. And there is much misuse of statistical tests – even in published journal articles.

In many small-scale research projects, simple summary or descriptive statistics convey much of the information you need. When supported by tables, bar charts and other displays of your data, they go a long way towards providing what you need to form the basis of your interpretation and to assist the reader in understanding your findings and their value. However, if there is an expectation in your field of study that you carry out complex statistical procedures, that is what you have to do, seeking advice where necessary.[§]

🕸 *The website (www.wiley.com/college/robson) gives links to material on quantitative analysis*

Qualitative Data

Many projects involve the collection of some qualitative, non-numerical data, most probably in the form of words. Responses to questions in interviews, notes that you make when observing and documents are three very common situations producing verbal outcomes. This may be a small contribution within an essentially quantitatively-oriented study. Or they may form the central features of your study.

Qualitative data aren't necessarily verbal – they can for example be visual, in the form of still or moving images: photographs, pictures, drawings, video, etc. Their analysis calls for specialized treatment (e.g. Banks, 2008).

Some qualitative data can be transformed into numbers. It can be possible and useful to develop a set of categories, work out which category a verbal response falls into and then count the frequency (i.e. the number of times) different categories are used. Such transformed data can then be summarized and displayed using the methods discussed in the previous section on quantitative data analysis.

However, much verbal data has a richness and complexity which cannot be captured by such processes. The challenge is to find ways of dealing with qualitative data which do them justice. One problem is that there is no single agreed way of going about this. Alternatives abound, typically linked to particular views about the kind of theoretical stance to adopt. It is not feasible to do justice to even a small number of these approaches in this kind of text (see Further Reading for references).

Most approaches, however, depend on finding ways of reducing and organizing the data.

[§] Steven Gorard, in an inspirational short book on using everyday numbers effectively in research (Gorard, 2006), makes a strong case for staying very simple when analysing numerical data.

Data reduction and organization

Qualitative data, whether interview transcripts, notes from observational sessions, or whatever, tend to be voluminous. To get a grip on what you have, you almost always need to reduce its volume, to organize and condense it into something more manageable. In carrying out this whole data reduction and organization process, take care not to distance yourself from the original data. The interpretation and understanding of qualitative data can be crucially dependent on their context.

In one sense, you have already done a major job of 'anticipatory' data reduction at the design stage of your study, by the choices you make about 'who', 'when' and 'where'. You only obtain data from a limited number of people, at specified times, and in particular places, determined by your research questions and the resources at your disposal.

Editing. Once you have some data, its reduction to something you can deal with is an important part of the data analysis. You edit out 'dross' – sections of interviews where respondents go off on an irrelevant topic, discarding irrelevant documents. Don't throw such stuff away though. You may find that your focus changes so that something becomes relevant in the future.

Summarizing. Producing summaries is invaluable. It not only reduces the amount of data, but producing the summary forces you to attend to the material closely. Keep the full data, of course; you may need verbatim (word for word) quotations for your account.

Coding. This involves splitting the data into units or segments that seem to you to be relevant and meaningful. You are looking for small chunks of material which might be put into categories, which can be provisionally labelled or named. And for wider themes and patterns which help organize the categories. This system may be derived from the data themselves, perhaps combined with categories and themes suggested by your previous reading and the research questions. The basic strategy is to compare and contrast – to find those things which seem to be similar and those which seem to be different. Be prepared to modify and change the categories and the way you organize them. You must retain flexibility as you acquire more data and/or develop different insights about what you have.

Memoing. This means writing memos to yourself reflecting insights, thoughts, and hunches about the data. This not only helps to understand what you have got but also to ensure you don't forget things. Memos also provide a useful record to show the process you have followed in dealing with the data.

Conceptualizing. At a later stage, the move is to conceptualize what you have found. How can the themes and patterns, which may change as more data are analysed, best be understood?

Figure 5.5 Matrix of issues and concerns by phase and level

Level	Phase				
	A	B	C	D	E
Local authority					
Head and senior management					
Class teachers					
Mentors					
Students					
Parents					

Displaying. As with quantitative data, displays of various kinds are a powerful way of reducing and organizing qualitative data. These include matrices, the equivalent of cross-tabulation, where two lists are set up as the rows and columns of a table. Figure 5.5 gives an example. The columns represent a sequence of stages in a project focusing on facilitating the entry of socially and economically disadvantaged students into university education. The rows cover different levels in the school system where the project was involved. The matrix provides a means of condensing much information from field notes into a single display. Supposing that matrices were produced for each of three case study schools, then this facilitates comparisons of the similarities and differences between the contexts.

Other possible displays include flow-charts and networks illustrating relationships and structures, typically by showing boxes and connections between them. The following section goes into more detail about one widely-used approach to the analysis of qualitative data.

An example – the grounded theory approach to analysis

Grounded theory is both an overall theoretical approach to doing research (seeking theory which is 'grounded' in, or derived from, the data you have collected) and a set of procedures for data analysis and interpretation.

It is essentially a three-step procedure. *Open coding* comes first – it is open in the sense of 'opening up' the data, splitting it up into small chunks and labelling (coding) them. You give the same label to those chunks which seem to be conceptually similar. A distinctive feature of the grounded theory approach is that right from the start you are looking for abstract, theoretical categories which help you to make sense of the data. The 'What is going on here?' question is up front. The codes or labels are provisional. You may need to change them as you obtain, and analyse, more data.

There is much to be said for doing this with a colleague, perhaps someone who also has qualitative data to analyse, so that you can help them out later. It helps to keep you honest, through having to defend your coding to a critical friend, and you can spark ideas off each other. If this isn't feasible, you should go through your analyses in detail afterwards with someone.

At this open coding stage, you should alternate between detailed, intensive scrutiny of sections of the data and a standing back to try to keep in mind the bigger picture. This will not only help to confirm or modify your thoughts about what the appropriate categories are, but also start to give ideas about how the individual categories might be grouped together and classified, and (the overall goal of grounded theory) what might be the core high-level category central in the data.

The second step is referred to as *theoretical coding*. Here, the task is to find ways of inter-relating the various categories produced through open coding. There are major disagreements between different proponents of grounded theory about how this should be done. The purist wing insist that these codes must emerge solely from study of the data. Others take a more relaxed view. My own preference is to acknowledge that it is difficult if not impossible (and probably undesirable anyway) to approach this task with a totally open mind. Your 'previous', i.e. what you bring to the analysis through prior reading and experience, and in particular your research questions, necessarily predispose you to look for particular kinds of relationships.

The final step is *selective coding*. This involves deciding on a core category. What is the central focus around which we can best integrate the data? Details and examples are provided in Corbin and Strauss (2008).

Grounded theory, though widely used, is just one of a plethora of approaches to the analysis of qualitative data – see Further Reading.

Using specialist computer packages for qualitative data analysis

There are several specialist packages which can help you make use of a computer to carry out an analysis of qualitative data. A system known as NVivo (http://www.qsrinternational.com/products_nvivo.aspx) is currently widely used but this is a field with rapid change. Whereas using statistical software such as SPSS with quantitative data is recommended for complex statistical analyses, whether or not to go for computer-assisted qualitative data analysis is a more difficult decision.

It is only worthwhile if you have a substantial amount of qualitative data to analyse and you are prepared to devote a considerable amount of time to gain facility in using the software. It is particularly worthwhile if you are going on to other projects producing qualitative data, and/or consider it a useful addition to your CV.

NVivo and other packages are essentially aids to carrying out the tasks you would be doing for yourself if you were completing the analysis by hand (working with interview transcripts, documents or whatever, coding and labelling different segments, sorting them out in various ways using highlighters, cutting, pasting, etc.). You don't, as it were, push a button and find the answer magically printed out as you do with SPSS. The software helps you to carry out the various tasks more systematically and provides various aids to displaying and summarizing your findings.

Summary of qualitative data analysis

Following the above principles should help you produce a worthwhile analysis. The procedure cannot be made routine in the kind of way that a statistical analysis of quantitative data can. Hence, it is a challenging task and can be daunting. It is very helpful to have advice and support from someone who has experience with this type of analysis.

The good news (and the bad news) is that there is no single 'right way' of doing qualitative data analysis. Take with a pinch of salt the advice of those who say that 'You must use X' – where X is ethnomethodology, or discourse analysis, or deconstruction, or the grounded theory approach focused on here. By all means, buy into a particular theoretical perspective and analytic system if you understand it and if it fits in with the purposes of your project.

Providing that you have approached the analysis in a systematic and disciplined manner and that you have provided sufficient detail so that a reader can get an answer to the question 'How did she get from these data to these conclusions?', you are in the clear.

> *The website (www.wiley.com/college/robson) gives links to material on qualitative analysis*

Interpretation – What is Going on Here?

This text emphasizes the importance of coming up with a small number of specific research questions, and of designing your project so that you are in a position to get answers to these questions. However, underlying the vast majority of projects lurks a more general or fundamental question: 'What is going on here?' 'How do I interpret, understand or explain the findings of my project?'

This is most obviously the central overarching question when the project has an explicit explanatory purpose. It is still on the agenda when the project is descriptive or exploratory. Suppose you have a research question which concerns the relative numbers of boys and girls with particular types of special needs (such as, for example, learning or behaviour difficulties) in schools and you find that there are more boys than girls with such needs in the schools you survey. Incidentally, international statistics commonly find an approximate 60% male to 40% female split (e.g. OECD, 2004; pp. 109–113). You might carry out an exploratory study where such a finding arises from your involvement in schools. While this information is valuable in its own right, raising issues about equity and the distribution of scarce resources, the 'What's going on here' question is inescapable.

Several possibilities might be suggested. Perhaps boys are more vulnerable than girls. It is known that certain disabilities are sex-linked, with boys more likely to be affected than girls. A very different explanation comes from suggestions that schooling is being increasingly 'feminized' (with, particularly at primary level, an increasing scarcity of male teachers) such that boys find it more difficult to fit in with the prevailing ethos. This might then lead to boys exhibiting more behavioural problems in the classroom – and being labelled as having 'special needs'. Another school-related factor might be linked to increased emphases being placed on the need for academic learning in schools in countries such as the United Kingdom where the position of schools in academic league tables is highly visible. Girls might outperform boys in areas such as literacy, resulting in boys again being judged as having special needs because of learning difficulties. A different social or cultural explanation might be that a society places more emphasis on the education of boys and hence their needs are given priority.

The philosophical stance known as *realism* provides a useful language for talking about these issues. The possibilities or factors discussed above are referred to as 'mechanisms'. Unfortunately, mechanism is viewed as something of a dirty word in some social research and other quarters. When the word is seen as meaning the 'construction of a machine', this view is understandable. However, the dictionary definition as 'an arrangement or action by which a result is obtained' is less provocative. Similarly 'mechanistic explanations' carry negative connotations whereas the meaning is simply 'explanations in terms of mechanisms'. The term is not really important. Substitute 'factor' or another synonym if 'mechanism' grates on you. However, the quest for an answer to the 'Why?' question is important. Realism provides this emphasis. It also stresses that realist mechanisms are 'underlying', that you are not limited to talking about things that can be directly observed and that one shouldn't expect mechanisms to operate for all situations or contexts, or for all people involved in a particular intervention. When studying some social situation, innovation, intervention or whatever, it is often not helpful or appropriate to be looking for general overall effects. What you are after is 'what works, for whom, and in what context' (Pawson & Tilley, 1997).

Because applied social research, in fields such as evaluation, has been plagued by weak, commonly inconsistent, overall findings, this changed perspective provides a welcome lifeline.

Realism stresses that mechanisms can operate at different levels, including the biological, psychological, social and societal levels. Thus, in the educational example given previously, biological mechanisms may well be effective in relation to specific disabilities. Psychological, individual person-level mechanisms may operate, resulting in emotional or behavioural difficulties being expressed. School and classroom climate may reflect the operation of social or group mechanisms, while societal mechanisms may result in differential priorities being given to male and female education.

To which you might legitimately complain that this is so complicated that I'm never going to be able to sort out what mechanisms or factors are operating in a particular study. Anything involving people (i.e. all social research, whether pure or applied) is inherently complicated.

Don't despair. The task becomes more manageable when you appreciate that you are not being asked to come up with definitive, copper-bottomed answers from a small-scale project. Science, particularly social science, isn't like that. Even the best designed and executed project can only, at best, help put 'another brick in the wall'. That is, it has to be seen in the context of other research and, generally, what is known and understood about a particular field or topic.

The good news is that, with sufficient thought, ingenuity and persistence, it ought to be possible to say something sensible about 'what's going on here' after any even half-way reasonable project. What is at issue is how plausible and believable a tale you can tell. Some designs make this task easier. If you already have a good idea about what is going on from previous research, or the views and experience of people who have been closely involved, then you can carry out a closely focused study putting your ideas to the test. An experimental design might be called for in this situation.

However, we often don't have the degree of pre-knowledge about these matters which would make an experiment a good bet. Or the situation might not lend itself to the degree of control needed in experimentation. Or your specific research questions, or the kind of project which you feel comfortable undertaking, could rule out experiments.

Further Reading

Bazeley, P. (2013). *Qualitative data analysis: Practical strategies*. London: Sage.
Clear, practical guide to all aspects of the analysis of qualitative data.

Corbin, J.M., & Strauss, A.C. (2008). *Basics of qualitative research: Techniques and procedures for developing grounded theory* (3rd ed.). Thousand Oaks, CA.: Sage.
Highly accessible text for doing a grounded theory project. Covers all aspects from developing research questions to different approaches to coding and analysis.

Field, A. (2013). *Discovering statistics using IBM SPSS statistics* (4th ed.). London: Sage.
Very impressive and accessible large text if you have to get to grips with statistical analysis. Note that this is a Kindle e-book edition.

Gibbs, G.R. (2002). *Qualitative data analysis: Explorations with NVivo*. Buckingham, Bucks.: Open University Press.
Covers the use of NVivo with several approaches to qualitative analysis including grounded theory. Clearly and logically presented.

Langdridge, D., & Hagger-Johnson, G. (2013) *Introduction to research methods and data analysis in psychology* (3rd ed.). Harlow, Essex: Pearson.
Part 2 provides clear coverage of a wide range of types of quantitative data analysis. Part 3 examines several approaches to the analysis of qualitative data, including phenomenological, grounded theory, discourse analysis, life story and narrative.

Pawson, R. (2013). *The science of evaluation: A realist manifesto*. London: Sage.
Chapter 6 provides what the author calls a Cook's tour of the place of mechanisms in studying interventions. One of the most stimulating writers about social research on top form.

Robson, C. (1994). *Experiment, design and statistics in psychology*. (3rd ed.). London: Penguin.
Covers simple statistical tests and ways of summarizing quantitative data. Full text available free from www.wiley.com/college/robson.

Salkind, N.J. (2013). *EXCEL statistics: A quick guide*. (2nd ed.). Thousand Oaks, CA.: Sage.
Shows how to use EXCEL to do a good range of statistical tests.

Note: Computer packages for both quantitative and qualitative data analysis regularly appear in revised and updated versions. The principles of NVivo and SPSS packages are likely to remain the same but you may have to use on-line manuals to cover new features.

Chapter 5 Tasks

Note: Following a flexible design, much of your data is likely to be qualitative in the form of words, but there are usually some numbers to be dealt with. A fixed design typically generates quantitative data in the form of numbers but can benefit from the use of a secondary data collection method which may well generate some words.

Where permitted by course regulations, seek help and advice with carrying out the following tasks:

1 *Decide how you will handle the quantitative data.* Decide on what are appropriate ways of dealing with the quantitative data you have collected. In all cases, you need to know how to summarize and display these data. You may need to carry out statistical tests, particularly in fixed design research.

2 *If you propose using statistical tests, familiarize yourself with SPSS (or another statistical analysis package).* Make sure that you know not only how to enter data and run the analysis, but also that you understand what the output means. Check this by running the analysis with fictitious data based on the results of your pilot.

3 *Decide how you will handle the qualitative data.* Small amounts of such data do not call for sophisticated treatment, but if you have a substantial amount, use some system (e.g. the grounded theory approach) for coding and interpreting the data. Make sure you understand what it involves.

4 *Decide whether or not you are going to use NVivo (or some other package) to analyse your qualitative data.* If you are, you need to familiarize yourself with the package.

5 *Go through these tasks before the main data collection exercise.* You don't want to be faced with a lot of data you don't know what to do with.

6

Reporting the Findings

The advice presented in earlier chapters was to make a start by writing drafts of parts of the report early in the research process. The most obvious bit to start on is the one giving the background to your choice of topic and discussion of relevant existing material and research – often called the 'literature review'. Once you have made decisions about the general approach to be taken, the research design and data collection methods, a start can also be made on these aspects – sometimes referred to as the 'methodology' chapter. Similarly, you will need to have given serious thought to the possible ethical issues raised by your project before data collection starts, so this can be discussed.

Any writing of this kind is good psychologically. You can see that progress is being made. Almost inevitably, you will be close to deadlines for completion of the project at the end, so material you can accumulate earlier helps. However, be prepared to re-draft (probably several times). Your findings and their interpretation will usually mean that the earlier stages have to be revisited in order to make sure that they 'fit'. Many people find it difficult to delete sections which are no longer relevant. However, just because you have written something doesn't mean it has to be in the final version of the report.

There can also be advantage in producing tentative drafts of the later parts of the report where you provide an interpretation of your findings, before you have completed the data collection and analysis. This is, of course, not an invitation to invent fictitious results. Researchers often have a pretty good idea about what the findings will be (or perhaps have two or three likely scenarios of what they will find). Writing up an interpretation will help you judge the strength or weakness of your research argument. It will also help to make apparent any gaps which need to be plugged by collecting additional data, or completing additional analyses.

Planning and Drafting

I am sure that although this might be your first research report, it won't be your first report or written assignment. While there are some specific features of research reports, which are covered below, good reports of whatever kind share common features. They are:

☐ clearly structured
☐ lucidly written
☐ professionally presented (which includes standard spelling, punctuation and referencing), and
☐ your own work.

As with any transition in the research process, there is a tendency to procrastinate when faced with the report-writing task. I'll start next week. I really ought to read a few more books, journal articles, other reports, etc., etc. Or I'm sure that I could get more out of my data if I kept working at them. Or I would do a better quality job if I had a short holiday. Or . . . All of which may have some truth but if you don't start, you don't finish. So give yourself a realistic deadline which will leave sufficient time to make a good job of the report. You will never be perfectly prepared to write, but you must give yourself the chance of making the best of what you have got.

Different people approach the task of writing the research report in different ways. However, everyone should have a plan of some kind before starting to write. The issue is whether to just have something very sketchy, or something on which you spend a lot of time trying to get the structure down in considerable detail. If you feel more secure following the latter path, then fine. However, it can be another ruse to put off the writing itself. And if you do go for a detailed plan, it is important to be prepared to modify it as you go on. Box 6.1 shows a general structure appropriate for many projects. Course handbooks usually include guidelines on the structure and type of presentation expected, including length. See if you can get hold of examples of recent project reports to get a feel for what others in your situation have done. Some institutions maintain archives of undergraduate projects or dissertations in printed or electronic format, typically with access restricted to registered students.

A plan helps a writer to jump the 'getting started' hurdle. At least you have a heading, not just a blank page or screen staring back at you. And if you are stuck with one section, it's always possible to turn to another one. There is, of course, no rule which says you have to proceed in a linear fashion, following section 1 with section 2, etc. Why not start by writing a section where you have a pretty strong notion of how you are going to treat it? As discussed above, it

Box 6.1 A possible report structure

1 *Title page* Title, including subtitle. Your name and date.
2 *Acknowledgments* Acknowledge the help you have received (don't forget to mention a helpful supervisor!).
3 *Contents* List the section headings and subheadings, giving their page numbers. Also provide a list of any figures or tables, and of any appendices, again with page numbers.
4 *Abstract* See p. 139. Keep to any word limits.
5 *Introduction* What you have done in the project, why and how. Give a brief background and the ethical issues, the research questions and the limitations of the study.
6 *Literature review* Gives the context of, and background to, your study. The review covers relevant previous research.
7 *Methodology* Details the general approach taken, the design of the project, the choice of methods and the ethical issues raised and how they were dealt with. In fixed design research, it is expected that sufficient detail is provided for a reader to carry out an exact replication of your study.
8 *Results* Presents the data and provides an analysis and interpretation of your findings.
9 *Discussion* Gives your answers to the research questions and a general discussion about the project and your findings. Includes relations to earlier findings, limitations, implications, improvements and suggestions for further research. If appropriate give recommendations for change and for the dissemination of the findings.
10 *References* Provides a full list of all works referred to in the report. See p. 139.
11 *Appendices* Includes copies of questionnaires and other research instruments (samples only) and any other relevant material (e.g. transcripts of interviews).

Note: Check if a particular structure is expected on your course. Use that structure. Regard the above as an aide-mémoire of things to include at some point in the report.

is comforting to have something, at least provisionally, in the bag. When you get a full draft, you are going to have to revisit sections you wrote at an early stage to make sure that everything fits together – probably deleting some parts you were initially quite proud of because they don't fit in with the way things turned out.

Given some kind of plan, my own preference is to 'splurge' when writing; i.e. to get stuck into the task and try to keep the words coming at a good rate, not worrying at this stage about style, clarity, spelling, punctuation. Others are unhappy with this strategy, preferring to try to produce a pretty clean draft version as they are writing.

When starting to plan your research report, you should have your research questions in front of you, literally as well as metaphorically. They may still be the original ones you started out with when preparing for your project as covered in Part I of this text. Quite possibly they will have changed and developed along the way. You should also have some, at least tentative, answers to these questions from the analysis of your data.

Some people like the security of having the structure of their report sorted out at quite an early stage. There is nothing wrong with this and it can help with time-planning. However, you should be prepared to revisit the structure, as well as the content, as you get a clearer idea of what you are getting out of the research data. Also, with a flexible design, you will be carrying out some data analysis and interpretation along the way, to help decide how later data collection goes. An account of this process is a legitimate contribution to the report. It helps readers to understand the journey you have taken when doing the project, and strengthens the trustworthiness of your findings.

Whatever your design, there will be elements of your report which you can work on almost from day one of your involvement in the project. There are usually times when you find that you can't make progress on data collection, perhaps because you are waiting for an approval of some kind. Or where you get fed up with working on analysing data. As the old adage goes, 'a change is as good as a rest'.

Research Arguments

When writing a research report, you are essentially presenting an argument (in the sense of evidence or proof, rather than a dispute). Booth, Colomb & Williams (2008; section III) suggest that there is a common set of elements to all research arguments – claims, reasons and evidence.

Claims

A doctoral 'thesis' is, strictly speaking, the main claim made in a dissertation. A common question at the oral examination is: 'So what, exactly, is your thesis?' The candidate is expected to come up with a sentence or two explaining the main claim that their dissertation supports.

In an undergraduate degree research report, while you can similarly end up with a main claim, it is likely that you will make several related claims. Following the research question route, these are your answers to these questions. One of the advantages of thinking in terms of research questions is that it keeps you focused on the claims you are going to be making.

Any research report should also be stuffed throughout with what might be called *mini-claims*. For example, in producing a literature review or review of previous research, you make a range of claims about what the previous work shows, how it can be understood, why and how it is relevant to your own research. When interpreting the data that you have analysed, you again come up with a range of claims for which you have to demonstrate support. In getting to the stage of providing answers to your research questions, there are likely to be several underlying claims to be evaluated.

Reasons and evidence

In its simplest form you:

[make a claim] because of [a reason].

For example, I read in newspapers at the time of writing that the childcare minister last week claimed that the French system of nursery education was superior to the system used in the UK because '[a]ll of their classes are structured and led by teachers'.

The distinctive feature of research is the requirement to provide the evidence, usually in the form of data, on which the reason is based. In other words, you:

[make a claim] because of [a reason] based on [evidence].

Here we have a claim of superiority, with a reason based on difference in approach and the evidence the minister cites is that '[w]hat you notice in French nurseries is just how calm they are', while children in British nurseries 'run around with no sense of purpose'. Clearly this is anecdotal evidence not put forward as a research finding, although there does seem to be an attempt to influence educational policy.

Supposing that you had been interested in the effects and effectiveness of nursery education and considered basing your project on this topic. While your interest might have been fired by your involvement at one or more nurseries or pre-schools in your own country or elsewhere you would, I am sure, have chased up sources of research on the topic. And there is good research evidence on the effectiveness of pre-school education (including nursery schools) in the UK from a major longitudinal study, 'Effective Provision of Pre-school Education (EPPE)' (Sylva, Melhuish, Sammons, Siraj-Blatchford & Taggart, 2010). This showed the 'quality of staff' as a key mechanism (explanatory factor, if you prefer) – that is, staff with higher qualifications, staff with leadership skills, long-serving staff, and trained teachers working alongside and supporting less-qualified staff. Interestingly, the French system requires high qualifications from their teaching staff in nursery schools whereas the UK system doesn't. Obviously this does not rule out the possibility of high-quality staff being more likely to have a structured curriculum and teacher-led sessions with this being the active mechanism. Alternatively, it could be that high-quality staff get superior results using their professional judgment about the environment best for their children.

A large project like EPPE can provide convincing evidence for these claims. Such claims from a single small-scale project are necessarily more tentative. Your responsibility is to make this clear and to not only repeat the old chestnut that 'more research needs to be done' but also to point a possible way forward. You should be wary of over-claiming the importance of your findings. However, take heart that the reliability and validity of the results of a well-designed and carried out research project far outweigh politically-driven anecdotal musings. As discussed on p. 142, you have a responsibility to disseminate your findings, particularly any which have 'real world' relevance. It is utopian to expect that policies, services or practices become evidence-based overnight, but you could make a difference.

You are inevitably selective in the reasons you cite and the evidence you use. It is necessary to cover alternatives. This is relatively easier when these are reasons that you have discarded or evidence that you have discounted. You say why you have done this to justify your choices. The difficult part is to try to anticipate other alternatives which you have not thought about. This is best dealt with by having colleagues critique drafts of your report, where you have given them the task of suggesting alternative explanations.

Considering Your Audience(s) – Again

Presenting the research argument can be thought of as a conversation with the reader of your report. The audience for a research report is usually considered to be those working in the field or discipline that your research focuses on. Not specialists in the particular topic of your study, but those with a general background and interest in education, nursing, social psychology, or wherever your focus lies. For an undergraduate research project, your direct audience is the people who are going to examine it. In practice, degree regulations often refer to a specific model of a research report or journal article. So that tells you what to aim at.

Consideration of audience expectations should influence your report's style and content. A simple strategy is to find a model (or preferably a few different ones) in the form of existing reports from students on your course in past years. If possible, select ones where there is evidence that it is highly regarded – perhaps your supervisor recommends them.

As discussed in Chapter 1, p. 11, you may be trying to reach other audiences as well as this main one. It may be necessary to provide a separate report for them, though you should be able to use material from your main report. For a study in an organization, the audience might be the managing director or personnel manager. For a report on a local initiative, the team running it. This will influence the approach you take and, importantly, the language and length of the report, but your job is essentially the same. You are making clear what you are claiming. Or, put in other terms, what your findings are. And you are providing reasons, with evidence, supporting your claim.

In a situation where secondary audiences of this kind just want to focus on the findings, or even on recommendations arising from them, there is nothing wrong with giving them what they ask for. You should have gone though the hard slog of following through the full research argument to ensure that you are making a justifiable claim when writing the report for the degree. If you have been given financial or other support, a good strategy is to supply an executive summary on one sheet, followed by a very short report, and then include your main report as an appendix. This makes it clear that you have done a lot of work.

If you wish to communicate to (and, hopefully, influence) other second audiences of non-academics, a formal report may well not be effective. Audiences, such as participants in your research, or clients of a service or innovation you were researching, might best be approached less formally, perhaps by a presentation of some kind, or production of a short newsletter. If you made a commitment to do this when negotiating access, make sure that you honour that commitment.

Some applied courses may expect you to provide evidence that you have sought to disseminate your findings (see p. 142). Including details of any presentations, newsletters, etc. in addition to your main report is one way of doing this.

Avoiding Plagiarism

Plagiarism, the passing off of someone else's work as you own, is a hot topic now that there is easy accessibility of all sorts of material via the internet.

While you are expected to hunt out relevant material from there, as well as printed materials in libraries, suggestions from supervisors or colleagues, or wherever, it is crucial that you acknowledge where all such material came from.

If you use a quotation (i.e. you copy an exact form of words), this has to be in quotation marks, with an attribution giving where, what and who it came from. If you are summarizing material, or taking an idea or finding from any source, you must also say what the source was.

You get credit from showing that you have read widely and that what you are saying is in some way linked to, and developed from, what others have done. Obviously a review of previous research which is simply a set of quotations from others, or a list of names of previous researchers and summaries of what they found, is deficient. You need to weave such material into the argument that you are presenting.

> The website (www.wiley.com/college/robson) gives links to material on avoiding plagiarism

Professional Standards

Most course regulations now require word-processed project reports. You are strongly advised to do this even if it is not a course requirement. A well-presented printed report looks professional and almost inevitably influences the reader in your favour. Anyhow, typing and word-processing skills are worth acquiring.

> The website (www.wiley.com/college/robson) gives links to material on the presentation of reports

Language matters

There is a tradition, in writing for scientific journals, of adopting a very impersonal language style (past tense, passive voice, e.g. 'subjects were asked to . . . '). If your course regulations expect this, then do this, though bear in mind that 'participants' is now preferred to 'subjects' in most disciplines (see Chapter 4, p. 86). Several reputable journals have now relaxed their rules on language style. If you have greater freedom regulation-wise, then choose a style which you prefer. It is common for reports of flexible design studies to use the active voice and to use the past tense only when describing things which did happen in the past. Again, look for project reports from your course in previous years and use them as a model.

Sexist, racist and disablist language is to be avoided in research reports. Apart from the insensitivity it displays and the offence that such language can cause, unthinking use of, say, a term such as 'businessman' for both males and females can cause confusion.

🕸 *The website (www.wiley.com/college/robson) gives links to material on avoiding sexist, racist and disablist language*

References

Examiners are likely to treat the quality of your referencing as an index of whether or not your work reaches the required professional standard. There are conventions about referencing which differ from discipline to discipline, with the APA (American Psychological Association) style required in several areas of social science research (see the discussion in Chapter 3, p. 69), Check what is expected and make sure that you follow the appropriate model closely. Obvious defects are where there is a mismatch between references in the text and the list of references at the end. Some in-text references may have been omitted from the list at the end. Or they may differ in some way, perhaps in dates or the spelling of authors' names. Some in the list may not appear in the text. Sorting this out can be a pain but it just requires time and effort rather than any deep thought.

How many references? This is something of a 'How long is a piece of string?' question. Don't assume that more is better. Discerning readers (which will include examiners) are going to spot if you are peppering your report with unnecessary references. Relevant previous research should be referenced but if it's a heavily researched area, you only need to select some good examples. Any claims or assertions should be referenced where feasible. If you reference some specific point with a book or long article, it's good practice to include the relevant page number(s). Don't reference things you haven't read. If you can't get hold of something you want to refer to which you find mentioned by someone else, you can do this as 'Bloggs (2003), as cited in Robinson (2005), claims that . . . .'.

Abstracts and executive summaries

An abstract is a short summary of the project, usually included at the beginning of the report. Its exact position and length is likely to be specified in the course regulations which, as always, you disobey at your peril. It should cover what you did, why this is of interest and importance, and what you have found. There is sometimes a requirement to include some key terms giving the main topics covered in the project. A common failing is to describe the project without summarizing the findings.

You can have a go at producing an abstract any time that you are clear about your findings. However, its definitive version is best left as the absolutely final task when writing the report. This abstract should be a polished jewel and it is worth spending time on getting it right.

It is important because the abstract is probably the first thing that the reader turns to, after noting the project title. Halo effects are almost inevitable. If there are spelling mistakes, clumsy sentences or non-sentences, or anything which gives a negative impression in the mind of the reader, this will colour their approach to the rest of the report. If it impresses positively, you are off to a good start.

The First Full Draft

Completing the first full draft is an important milestone in writing the report. To achieve this, you need to be able to concentrate on writing and not let other tasks get in the way. There may be some additional work to be done in analysis and interpretation arising from the report as you are accumulating the chapters, but with the finishing post in sight your day-to-day task is writing. And, of course, making sure that you are keeping copies of what you are writing. Beware the curse of the computer as it prepares a hard disc crash to coincide with your completing the draft!

If you are stuck while writing, you have two choices. One is to keep writing regardless. You might be able to work your way through the block and produce something worthwhile. If you think what you have produced is pretty awful, mark it in the text as something you are going to have tò return to. The alternative when stuck is to tackle some other part of the report. By now, you won't have the luxury of taking a long break and hoping that inspiration will strike.

So, by hook or by crook you get to the full draft. Inevitably some bits will be worse than others. Don't worry overmuch about the weaker parts. You can attend to them while revising the draft.

Revising and Polishing

If you can produce a full draft, you are going to finish the project. The next phase, revising and polishing, helps ensure that you make the most of all your efforts in designing and carrying out the project.

In an ideal world, you would allow a week or two to elapse from completing the draft to trying to revise it. If deadlines loom, it's probably more realistic to think in terms of giving yourself the afternoon off, getting a good sleep, and turning to 'revise mode' bright-eyed and bushy-tailed the next morning.

When producing the first draft, you are telling your story of the project; effectively you are writing for yourself. When revising, you need to have the reader, metaphorically, looking over your shoulder as you review what you have written. Would someone else understand what I am getting at here? Do I need to add material so that they can follow the argument?

You also need to polish. Some sentences will be over-long, over-complex and poorly expressed. There will be repetition. You forgot that you had covered something earlier and say it twice. Some repetition is needed to help communication but reference back may be better. Everyone has their favourite words and phrases which they tend to overuse. Find out what yours are (you may have to get a friend to tell you) and seek alternatives. Is the tone right? Are you being condescending to the reader? Or inappropriately friendly? While, traditionally, scientific reports have been written in the rather forbidding linguistic code using passive constructions and the past tense with the voice of the researcher suppressed, you may not be constrained to that extent. Find out the expectations for your report. As ever, you play the game according to the rules set. If there is freedom in the way you can report, then choose whatever style seems best to communicate what you have done and found.

It makes sense to use a spelling checker. If nothing else, it will pick up inadvertent typos where what you have written wasn't what you intended. Remember that it won't pick up correctly spelled words (e.g. if you intended to write 'their' but typed 'there'). I don't like grammar checkers as I spend a large amount of time disagreeing with their suggestions. However, it's up to you. Professional presentation also includes having a standard system for headings and sub-headings in the report and for standard spacing between sections, sub-sections, etc. Find a model you like and follow it.

The Final Version

Try to get to what you consider the final version of the report a few days (at least) before the deadline for handing it in. Ask someone else to copy-edit it, i.e. to go through it with a fine-tooth-comb looking for any residual things which need tidying up. The spelling mistakes which a checker doesn't find, sentences which don't communicate well, punctuation, etc. At this stage, you don't want someone to be making serious criticisms of the substance of your report as you don't have the time to deal with them. Now is the time to call in a favour from a friend. Use bribery if necessary.

Disseminating Your Findings

It is a sad fact of life that the project report that you have laboured over is unlikely to be widely read. Your examiners may be the only ones to read it. If, as I hope and trust, you have done a worthwhile piece of work, you should seek other ways of disseminating your findings.

Oral presentations

Some course regulations call for other presentations of your findings as well as the project report. For example, this might be a short oral presentation in front of some staff and fellow students. This is a valuable exercise, as it is not only the type of thing which anyone following a research or academic career will find they have to do, but it is common in many other graduate job situations. Some institutions hold conferences where undergraduates make presentations – see, for example, papers by Andersen (2011), Bachmutsky (2011) and Mancini (2012) given at the University of California at Berkeley's annual conference.

The key to doing this well is to prepare and to rehearse. Make yourself familiar with PowerPoint and produce a slideshow covering the main points of your project and its findings. Use graphs and figures where possible. Go through it yourself and make sure you can complete the presentation in the time allocated. If at all possible, have a dummy run with a few colleagues. Prime them with some good questions to which you know the answers.

On the day, check that you are familiar with the equipment. Remember to face the audience and not just give them your back view. Remember also that your audience can read. You shouldn't spend most of the time just reading out the text on the slides.

Poster presentations are another format widely used at conferences and workshops and for some undergraduate degrees (Barker, 2011 provides an example, also from Berkeley's undergraduate conference). They can include rather more words than you would use for a slideshow, though you may use printouts of the slides together with additional information. Once again, pay serious attention to the standard of presentation. Some are truly awful.

As indicated on p. 136, some other form of presentation may be needed to fulfil the commitments you made to participants and others, while carrying out the research. This may be in the form of a slide presentation or a short leaflet tailored to the interests and backgrounds of those involved. You may be able to give further presentations to groups or organizations with interests in the topic of your project. Apart from publicizing your findings, it all gives you useful experience and adds to your CV.

Other types of publication

You should think of publishing an account of your project in an academic or professional journal, particularly if you are hoping to follow a career in one of those areas. In many such journals, it is common to have your supervisor(s) as a second author. They should certainly give you advice about the proposed paper and possible journals. The journals themselves give advice on their expectations. Don't be discouraged if you get a refusal. My first attempt as a student was turned down with a very negative review. My supervisor thought the comments unfair and his intervention was followed by acceptance for publication.

In recent years, several journals specifically publishing work by undergraduate students have appeared in various countries including the UK and North America. A range of examples was presented in Chapter 2, pp. 33–40 and 46–53.

Don't ignore having an account of your work published in a newspaper or specialist magazine. Busy reporters and editors often welcome copy that they can use without having to do much editing. You might even get a (small) fee.

The website (www.wiley.com/college/robson) gives links to material on disseminating your findings

A Final Thought

Don't be distressed if your efforts to spread the word about your findings and their interest, value or usefulness seem to fall on stony ground. It is too much to hope that your small-scale, first attempt at a research project is going to have much impact, if any. A few do, most don't. Your main aim has been to complete it, and to satisfy your examiners that it is of degree standard. Hence, the most important impact is on yourself. For some it will represent the first step in a research career. For many more it will have helped you develop a set of very marketable skills which can both improve your employability, and which can be further developed in the work context. For most it represents success with a rather daunting challenge. Congratulate yourself and all those who have helped you.

Further Reading

Becker, H.S. (2007). *Writing for social scientists: How to start and finish your thesis, book, or article* (2nd ed.). Chicago, IL.: University of Chicago Press.
   Clear and down-to-earth, written from a lifetime's experience.
Booth, W.C., Colomb, G.G., & Williams, J.M. (2008). *The craft of research* (3rd ed.). Chicago, IL.: University of Chicago Press.
   Part IV covers planning, drafting and revising a research report. A blend of wisdom and practical tips.

Chapter 6 Tasks

1 *Find out what your course regulations say about the report and its presentation*. This includes aspects such as format and structure, referencing system to be used, length (and whether appendices are to be included in the word count – usually they are not counted) and the deadline date for submission of the report.

2 *Find out whether the supervisor will comment on a draft of the report*. Practices vary on this. If they will comment, make sure you take this opportunity and take serious note of any comments or suggestions. Let them have it in time to read it and for you to act on suggestions before the deadline.

Now that you have gone through all the chapters, I hope that you have an appreciation of the main things to sort out in designing and delivering a quality project.

If you haven't already done so, now is a good time to have a go at the tasks listed in the previous chapters. They are best tackled following, more or less, the sequence in the book and before you get yourself into the main data collection phase.

References and Author Index

This list of references incorporates an author index. The numbers in **bold** at the end of each entry indicate where the publication is referred to in this book.

For many journal references the simplest method of accessing the reference is to type (or copy) the title into Google or another search engine. Journal websites have been given for e-journals and provide an alternative route (some give direct access to the article; for others you will have to select the article from those listed).

Akister, J., Williams, I., & Maynard, A. (2009). Using group supervision for undergraduate dissertations: A preliminary enquiry into the student experience. *Practice and Evidence of Scholarship of Teaching and Learning in Higher Education*, 4(2), 77-94. Retrieved from http://hdl.handle.net/10540/115667 **14**

American Psychological Association. (2013). *Publication Manual of the American Psychological Association*. (6th ed.). Washington, DC.: American Psychological Association. **69, 86**

Andersen, C. (2011). User perceptions of hand sanitizer in water-constrained communities: A field study in Hubli. *Berkeley Undergraduate Journal*, 24(2), 5-11. Retrieved from http://escholarship.org/uc/item/2qd951sm **142**

Armstrong, A. (2008). Fluency and fun in Spanish through TPRS: An action research project. *UW-L Journal of Undergraduate Research*, 11, 1-6. Retrieved from http://www.uwlax.edu/urc/JUR-online/html/2008.htm **33**

Austin, C. (2010). Using knowledge interventions to determine stress and future preventative behaviour regarding cervical cancer and the human papilloma virus. *Diffusion, University of Central Lancashire*, 5(1). Retrieved from http://atp.uclan.ac.uk/buddypress/diffusion/?p=976 **38**

Bachmutsky, R. (2011). Home away from home: How birthright shapes the thought and discourse about Israel among American Jewish young adults. *Berkeley Undergraduate Journal,* 24(2), 66–74. Retrieved from http://escholarship.org/uc/item/0zr5v1n5 **142**

Banks, M. (2008). *Using visual data in qualitative research.* London: Sage. **122**

Bantle, E. (2010). Creating Patagonia National Park: Understanding community response to national park creation by a private foreign non-profit organization. *UW-L Journal of Undergraduate Research,* 12, 1–13. Retrieved from http://www.uwlax.edu/urc/JUR-online/html/2010.htm **35**

Barker, M. (2011). Kulia i ka nu'u: Native Hawaiian single mothers striving for excellence under the guise of welfare reform. *Berkeley Undergraduate Journal,* 24(2), 75–77. Retrieved from http://escholarship.org/uc/item/68c3856d **142**

Barth, M. (2008). A nutrition assessment of dietary practices of Mexicans living in the state of Veracruz. *UW-L Journal of Undergraduate Research,* 11, 1–4. Retrieved from http://www.uwlax.edu/urc/JUR-online/html/2008.htm **37**

Booth, W. C., Colomb, G. G., & Williams, J. M. (2008). *The craft of research* (3rd ed.). Chicago, IL.: University of Chicago Press. **134**

British Psychological Society. (2010). *Code of human research ethics.* Leicester, Leics: British Psychological Society. **86**

Chandy, R. (2008). Wikiganda: Identifying propaganda through text analysis. *Caltech Undergraduate Research Journal,* 9(1), 10–15. Retrieved from http://curj.caltech.edu/issues/ **70**

Co, G., & Nieri, T. (2012). Perceived division of labor and work-family conflict among U.S. married and cohabiting women in heterosexual couples. *University of California, Riverside: Undergraduate Research Journal,* 6, 5–11. Retrieved from http://ugr.ucr.edu/journal/volumes/volume6/ **52**

Coolican, H. (2014). *Research methods and statistics in psychology* (6th ed.). Hove, E. Sussex: Psychology. **67**

Croxford, A. M. (2010). An evaluation of routine screening, assessment and treatment of depression for patients on the diabetes and/or coronary heart disease registers in a primary care practice in Norfolk. *Reinvention: a Journal of Undergraduate Research,* 3(1) Retrieved from http://www.warwick.ac.uk/reinventionjournal/issues/volume3issue1/croxford/ **51**

Dale, L. (2013). How an early caregiving style affects adult romantic love. *Reinvention: an International Journal of Undergraduate Research,* 6(1) Retrieved from www.warwick.ac.uk/reinventionjournal/issues/volume6issue1/dale **48**

Dalrymple, L. C. (2009). Judging a book by its album cover: A study of the relationship between musical preference and personality. *Vanderbilt Undergraduate Research Journal,* 5(1), 1–10. Retrieved from journal website http://ejournals.library.vanderbilt.edu/index.php/vurj/article/view/2855 **49**

DeDeyn, R. (2008). A comparison of academic stress among Australian and international students. *UW-L Journal of Undergraduate Research*, 11, 1–4. Retrieved from http://www.uwlax.edu/urc/JUR-online/html/2008.htm **49**

Dewsnap, F., & Smart, A. (2011). The meanings of well-being and intuition in crystal therapy: A qualitative interview study. *Reinvention: Journal of Undergraduate Research*, 4(1). Retrieved from http://www.warwick.ac.uk/go/reinventionjournal/issues/volume4issue1/dewsnapsmart **47**

Driessen, C. E. (2005). Message communication in advertising: Selling the Abercrombie and Fitch image. *UW-L Journal of Undergraduate Research*, 8, 1–12. Retrieved from http://www.uwlax.edu/urc/JUR-online/html/2005.htm **35**

Dunbar, G. (2005). *Evaluating research methods in psychology: A case study approach*. Oxford, Oxon.: Blackwell. **60**

Entringer, T., & Starck, L. (2010). What's in a voice? Vocal characteristics and their influence on courtroom decision making. *UW-L Journal of Undergraduate Research*, 13, 1–4. Retrieved from journal website http://www.uwlax.edu/urc/JUR-online/html/2010.htm **47**

Farr, Z. (2012). A study of sexist attitudes among students. *IDEATE: the undergraduate journal of sociology*, 7, 1–11. Retrieved from http://www.essex.ac.uk/sociology/research/publications/student_journals/ug/vol7_spring2012.aspx **51**

Frampton, H. (2010). Exploring teenage pregnancy and media representations of 'chavs'. *Reinvention: a Journal of Undergraduate Research*, 3(1). Retrieved from www.warwick.ac.uk/go/reinventionjournal/issues/volume3issue1/frampton **52**

Fung, O. (2010). The construction of 'peoplehood' in the second wave of Norwegian black metal. *Reinvention: a Journal of Undergraduate Research*, 3(2). Retrieved from http://www.warwick.ac.uk/go/reinventionjournal/issues/volume3issue2/fung **39**

Goodman, A. (2009). Teen and adult activities onboard a cruise ship. *UW-L Journal of Undergraduate Research*, 13, 1–4. Retrieved from http://www.uwlax.edu/urc/JUR-online/html/2009.htm **47**

Gorard, S. (2006). *Using everyday numbers effectively in research*. London: Continuum. **122**

Grames, M., & Leverentz, C. (2010). Attitudes toward persons with disabilities: A comparison of Chinese and American Students. *UW-L Journal of Undergraduate Research*, 13, 1–6. Retrieved from http://www.uwlax.edu/urc/JUR-online/html/2010.htm **38**

Hakim, C. (2000). *Research design: Successful designs for social and economic research* (2nd ed.). London: Routledge. **22**

Harguth, J. (2010). Childhood obesity: The role of dairy products. *UW-L Journal of Undergraduate Research*, 13, 1–10. Retrieved from http://www .uwlax.edu/urc/JUR-online/html/2010.htm **37**

Harrison, M. E., & Whalley, W. B. (2008). Undertaking a dissertation from start to finish: The process and product, *Journal of Geography in Higher Education*, 32(3), 401–418. DOI: 10.1080/03098260701731173 **X**

Hirschberg, M. (2012). Living with chronic illness: An investigation of its impact on social participation. *Reinvention: a Journal of Undergraduate Research*, 3(2). *Retrieved from Reinvention: a Journal of Undergraduate Research*, 5(1), http://www.warwick.ac.uk/reinventionjournal/issues/volume5 issue1/hirschberg **69**

Hodgkiss, A., & Handy, C. (2007). The criminal face effect: Physical attractiveness and character integrity as determinants of perceived criminality. *Retrieved from Reinvention: a Journal of Undergraduate Research*, Launch Issue, http://www.warwick.ac.uk/go/reinventionjournal/ pastissues/launchissue/paper1 **37**

Hunn, D. (2009). The relationship between unemployment and communist-era legacies in Leipzig, Germany. *Reinvention: a Journal of Undergraduate Research*, 2(2). Retrieved from www.warwick.ac.uk/go/reinventionjournal/issues/volume2issue2/hunn **47**

Kanoun, N. (2009). Validation of the ActivPAL Activity Monitor as a measure of walking at pre-determined slow walking speeds in a healthy population in a controlled setting. *Reinvention: a Journal of Undergraduate Research*, 2(2). Retrieved from www.warwick.ac.uk/go/reinventionjournal/ issues/volume2issue2/kanoun **49**

Kelly, J. (2011). The ambitions of secondary school girls in Jinja district, Uganda in the context of 'gender balancing'. *GeoVerse* (ISSN: 1758-3411) September 2011. Retrieved from geoverse.brookes.ac.uk/article_resources/ kellyJ/Jinja-JK-Geoverse.pdf **77**

Kennedy, J. (2010). Image reparation strategies in sports: Media analysis of Kobe Bryant and Barry Bonds. *Retrieved from The Elon Journal of Undergraduate Research in Communications*, 1(1) 95–104. **34**

Kramer, M. (2012). The unravelling of apparel: Online shopping behaviour. *Reinvention: a Journal of Undergraduate Research*, 5(1), Retrieved from http:// www.warwick.ac.uk/reinventionjournal/issues/volume5issue1/kramer **48, 62, 69**

Lehtonen, M. (2009). The development of religious tolerance: Co-operative board games with children and adolescents. *Reinvention: a Journal of Undergraduate Research*, 2(2). Retrieved from http://www.warwick.ac.uk/ go/reinventionjournal/issues/volume2issue2/lehtonen **36**

Levine-Murray, A. (2012). Community and exclusion in the gay Mecca. *Berkeley Undergraduate Journal*, 25(3), 49–53. Retrieved from http://escho larship.org/uc/item/15k0c25d **51**

Li, H. C. (2010). Using podcasts for learning English: Perceptions of Hong Kong Secondary 6 ESL students. *Début: the Undergraduate Journal of Languages, Linguistics and Area Studies*, 1(2). Retrieved from http://www .studyinglanguages.ac.uk/student_voices/debut_autumn2010 **62**

Mancini, T. (2012). Understanding and self-advocacy: Students with learning disabilities, unrecognized talent. *Berkeley Undergraduate Journal*, 25(3), 100–109. Retrieved from http://escholarship.org/uc/item/6ph5w1q8 **142**

Marshall, L. (2009). Swaziland: A protective environment for children? Utilising and evaluating the UNICEF framework in a developing society. *Reinvention: a Journal of Undergraduate Research*, 2(2). Retrieved from http:// www.warwick.ac.uk/go/reinventionjournal/issues/volume2issue2/marshall **33**

Mayo, G. (2010). Nature in the city: Young people's perceptions, values and experiences. *Diffusion, University of Central Lancashire*, 5(1). Retrieved from http://atp.uclan.ac.uk/buddypress/diffusion/?p=935 **52**

McDonnell, S. (2011). How the sport education model supports the inclusion of children marginalised as lower ability in physical education, *Alfred: An undergraduate research journal*, 3, 37–42. Retrieved from http:// www.winchester.ac.uk/Studyhere/ExcellenceinLearningandTeaching/ research/e-journals/Pages/ALFRED.aspx **33**

McGivern, P., & Noret, N. (2011). Online social networking and e-safety: Analysis of risk-taking behaviours and negative online experiences among adolescents, *Reinvention: a Journal of Undergraduate Research*, British Conference of Undergraduate Research 2011 Special Issue. Retrieved from http:// www.warwick.ac.uk/go/reinventionjournal/issues/BCUR2011specialissue/ mcgivernnoret **36, 62**

Nguyen, A. (2011). Do you want the good news or the bad news first? News order influences recipients' mood, perceptions, and behaviors. *University of California, Riverside: Undergraduate Research Journal*, 5, 31–36. Retrieved from http://ugr.ucr.edu/journal/volumes/volume5/ **38**

OECD. (2004). *Equity in education: Students with disabilities, learning difficulties and disadvantages*. Paris: Organization for Economic Co-Operation and Development. **127**

Pawson, R., & Tilley, N. (1997). *Realistic evaluation*. London: Sage. **128**

Pesko, M. (2009). Investigation of Wisconsin's family care policy: Research and recommendations concerning employment outcomes for people with disabilities. *Reinvention: a Journal of Undergraduate Research*, 2(2). Retrieved from www.warwick.ac.uk/go/reinventionjournal/issues/ volume2issue2/pesko **48**

Petrus, E. R. (2007). Fighting the addiction: The effectiveness of the La Crosse County drug court program. *UW-L Journal of Undergraduate Research*, 10, 1–7. Retrieved from http://www.uwlax.edu/urc/JUR-online/html/2007.htm **39**

Quigley-Jones, J. (2012). Encouraging female entrepreneurship: Lessons from Colombian women. *Reinvention: an International Journal of Undergraduate Research*, 5(2). Retrieved from www.warwick.ac.uk/reinvention-journal/issues/volume5issue2/quigley-jones **36**

Raders, G. (2008). Combating the privatization of life in a neo-liberal regime: The fight for water democracies in India, *Berkeley Undergraduate Journal*, 22(1), 1–44. Retrieved from http://escholarship.org/uc/item/4d73n733 **33**

Roberts, S., Hine, C., Morey, Y., Snee, H., & Watson, H. (2013). *Digital methods as mainstream methodology: Building capacity in the research community to address the challenges and opportunities presented by digitally inspired methods.* Discussion Paper. NCRM. (Unpublished). Retrieved from http://eprints.ncrm.ac.uk/3156/ **3**

Robson, C. (2000). Small-scale evaluation: Principles and practice. London: Sage. **13**

Robson, C. (2011). *Real world research: A resource for users of social research methods in applied settings* (3rd ed.). Chichester, W. Sussex.: Wiley. **54**

Rodrigues, N. (2012). Easily frustrated infants: Implications for emotion regulation strategies and cognitive functioning. *Vanderbilt Undergraduate Research Journal*, 8, 1–7. Retrieved from http://ejournals.library.vanderbilt.edu/ojs/index.php/vurj/article/view/2928 **50**

Rosenberg, E. (2012). The National Association of Professional Base Ball Players: The origins of professional baseball and the American identity. *Vanderbilt Undergraduate Research Journal*, 8, 1–7. Retrieved from http://ejournals.library.vanderbilt.edu/ojs/index.php/vurj/article/view/3522 **40**

Scharf, E. (2010). Entitled to benefit? A review of state benefit take up by older people belonging to black and minority ethnic groups. *Reinvention: a Journal of Undergraduate Research*, 3(2). Retrieved from www.warwick.ac.uk/go/reinventionjournal/issues/volume3issue2/scharf **39**

Stach, W. (2007). Sister sister: Interpreting intimacy in sibling relationships. *UW-L Journal of Undergraduate Research*, 10, 1–15. Retrieved from http://www.uwlax.edu/urc/JUR-online/html/2007.htm **35**

Sutherland, R. S. (2012). 'The Scottish hate us more than the Muslims . . . ': The north/south divide? A comparative analysis of the agenda, activities and development of the English and Scottish Defence Leagues, *Reinvention: a Journal of Undergraduate Research*, British Conference of Undergraduate Research 2011 Special Issue. Retrieved from www.warwick.ac.uk/go/reinventionjournal/issues/bcur2012specialissue/sutherland **69**

Sylva, K., Melhuish, E. C., Sammons, P., Siraj-Blatchford, I., & Taggart, B. (2010). *Early childhood matters: Evidence from the effective pre-school and primary education project.* Abingdon, Oxon.: Routledge. **136**

Tadt, R. (2007). An evaluation of physical impacts in backcountry camping areas at Glacier national park. *UW-L Journal of Undergraduate Research*, 10, 1–4. Retrieved from http://www.uwlax.edu/urc/JUR-online/html/2007.htm **39**

Thornton, E. (2011). Linguistic habitus and the domination of Latino workers in the American restaurant industry: An ethnographic sketch. *Reinvention: a Journal of Undergraduate Research*, 4(1). Retrieved from http://www.warwick.ac.uk/go/reinventionjournal/issues/volume4issue1/thornton **34, 50**

Turtenwald, A. (2012). Physical intimacy and equity in the maintenance of college students' romantic relationships. *UW-L Journal of Undergraduate Research*, 15, 1–9. Retrieved from http://www.uwlax.edu/urc/JUR-online/html/2012.htm **53**

Upstill, A. (2011). Community gardens or gardening communities: A survey of community gardens on Austin's East Side. *The University of Texas at Austin Undergraduate Research Journal*, 10, 23–38. Retrieved from http://texasurj.com/archive/ **35**

Velasquez, N. (2012). Compartmentalization and poor marital outcomes: Are negative conflict resolution tactics to blame? *The University of Texas at Austin Undergraduate Research Journal*, 11, 82–95. Retrieved from http://texasurj.com/archive/ **50**

Vogelsinger, C. (2010). Twitter: a quantitative, semantic content analysis of the top 10 Twitter brands. *Diffusion, University of Central Lancashire*, 5(1). Retrieved from http://atp.uclan.ac.uk/buddypress/diffusion/?p=964 **52**

Wheatley, A. (2010). Donor insemination: The role of the internet in the experiences of donor offspring, DI parents and donors. *Reinvention: a Journal of Undergraduate Research*, 3(2). Retrieved from http://www.warwick.ac.uk/go/reinventionjournal/issues/volume3issue2/wheatley **36, 62**

Wilding, D. (2008). The educational experiences of gypsy travellers: The impact of cultural dissonance. *Reinvention: a Journal of Undergraduate Research*, 1(1). Retrieved from http://www2.warwick.ac.uk/go/reinventionjournal/volume1issue1/wilding **34**

Young, E. (2011). The impacts of educational attainment, professional interests, and residency on community involvement and civic engagement. *Colonial Academic Alliance Undergraduate Research Journal*, 2, Article 4. Retrieved from http://scholarworks.gsu.edu/caaurj/vol2/iss1/4 **34**

Subject Index